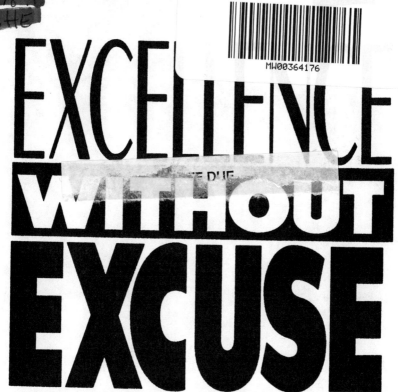

EXCELLENCE WITHOUT EXCUSE

THE BLACK STUDENT'S GUIDE TO ACADEMIC EXCELLENCE

CHARLES W. CHERRY II

INTERNATIONAL SCHOLASTIC PRESS

INTERNATIONAL SCHOLASTIC PRESS INC.
FORT LAUDERDALE FLORIDA

EXCELLENCE WITHOUT EXCUSE:

THE BLACK STUDENT'S
GUIDE TO
ACADEMIC EXCELLENCE

Published by International Scholastic Press, Inc., P.O. Box 238, Fort Lauderdale, FL 33302-0238. Street address: 121 NW 6th Avenue, Ft Lauderdale, FL 33311. Phone: (305) 527-4259. Fax: (305) 527-0223.

Typesetting by Daytona Times, Inc., Daytona Beach, FL and Resolutions, Ft. Lauderdale, FL.

Cover Design by Troy Brown Design, Oak Park, IL.

Library of Congress Cataloging-in-Publication Data

Cherry, Charles W. (Charles William), 1956 -
    Excellence without excuse: The Black Student's guide to academic excellence/by Charles W. Cherry II. — 1st ed. p. cm.
    Includes bibliographical references and index (p.) and index.
    ISBN 1-56385-497-X. -- ISBN 1-56385-498-8 (pbk.)
    1. Afro-Americans—Education (Higher) 2. Afro-American College students—Attitudes. 3. Academic achievement—United States. 4. Study, method of I. Title.

LC2781.C48   91-35248
378.1 '98296073-dc20   CIP

2 3 4 5 6 7 8 9 10

ACKNOWLEDGMENTS

Many people are at least partially responsible for whatever educational accomplishments I have made in my 25 years of formal schooling. Before I list them, I must first give thanks to God for continuing to pour out unmerited grace and favor upon me. It is my fervent prayer that this, my initial written offering to Him, be pleasing in His sight.

Thanks go to Mom, Dad, Glenn and Cassandra, my immediate family. Through them, I have learned that a whole, supportive, and loving family is really heaven on earth; to my beloved grandmother, the late Emma H. Troutman, perseverance personified; "when I get to heaven, I'll run to Grandma's hands." Thanks also to my Aunt Mable Barlow and my late Aunts Dufferin B. Harris and Leila Barlow, who whet my thirst for education and give me silent inspiration; to the Harper side of the family, particularly Dr. Charlyn Harper, who has always seen the W.E.B. DuBois in me; to the old Campbell Elementary School staff and faculty in Daytona Beach, including the late Mr. J.H. Dickerson, Mrs. Edna Barker-Washington, Mrs. Eula Gray, Mrs. Dorothy Moore and Mrs. Margaret McClairen; to Mrs. Ann Arcuri and Sr. Ann Francis of St. Paul's Catholic School.

To Mrs. Elizabeth McGhee and Coach Dick Edson at Seabreeze High; to Psi Chapter of the Omega Psi Phi Fraternity, Morehouse College; the Morehouse College track team, especially Ed Moses, and my fellow Morehouse Men who honed my competitive instincts; to the Clark College (now Clark-Atlanta University) Mass Communications Department, especially Nellie Dixon, who challenged my writing ability for the first time; to Drs. Atiase, Armstead, Brigham, Cornelius, Davis, Elnicki, Jermier, Mathjay, Popper, and Tosi, all present at the University of Florida's Graduate School of Business during my matriculation, and Prof. Walter Weyrauch of the University of Florida College of Law.

To Lamon Lampley and John Angus `Cho' Davis, my Black MBA/JD colleagues who helped keep the dream alive; to Adlancy Horne, UF's "Black Academic Godfather", and Kunle Ogundele, tutors without peer; to Brother Kenneth C. Jacobs, Sr., who knows the meaning of true brotherhood; and to Margaret Carey, who pulled my fat out of the academic fire at the law school more than once; and to the whole gang of Black undergraduate and graduate and professional students who attended UF from 1978 to 1982.

Special thanks go to some special sisters. Where would a Black man be without them? To Deetra Sands Durham, my silent (and sometimes not-so-silent) partner emotionally and intellectually through college, law school and business school; Sikita Laster Goodrich, whose pride in me and high expectations of me put me back on track academically; Natasha Williams, Esq., my bridge over troubled waters during the last semester and the Florida Bar Exam; Carmen Oliver Williamson, who always pushes me toward excellence; Koren DeLisser who kept the pressure on toward the end; and Cherryl Christie Cloyd who, in many unforeseen ways, helped me cross the finish line on this project.

Many folks also contributed to this book, maybe without knowing it. Thanks go to J. Allen Zow, Esq., my spiritual partner; Bro. Harry Harrell, my computer expert and a kindred spirit, and the brothers of Omega Psi Phi Fraternity, Eta Nu Chapter, Pompano Beach, FL; Jeby and Ron, for the software; and for all the people at the Broward County (Florida) Courthouse, who had encouraging as well as discouraging words. Thanks also to my brothers at the Bar: Charles Morton, Greg Durden, Johnny McCray, James DeHart, Michael Robinson, Theota McClaine.

Another special thanks to 100 Black Men of Broward County, Inc., an organization of Black men which is the real future of our community. I am proud to be a member. Also, many clients, including Dr. William H. Lindsey and the staff and management of the Housing Authority of the City of Fort Lauderdale, provided understanding and encouragement that allowed me to work and write. Last but not least, to the shareholders of Omega Diversified Investment Consortium and Psi Communications, Inc., who have, over the years, continued to believe in both Glenn and me. Brothers, our time has come!

God bless you all.

Charles W. Cherry II
June 1986 to October 1992

DEDICATION

To the three groups of African scholars: those who have gone before, those who are here today, and those who are yet to come...

EXCELLENCE WITHOUT EXCUSE: THE BLACK STUDENT'S GUIDE TO ACADEMIC EXCELLENCE

By Charles W. Cherry II, B.A., J.D., M.B.A.

TABLE OF CONTENTS

   A. Common Assumptions Blacks Make About Whites:
      1. whites are smarter than Blacks, and always know what they are doing
      2. white folks are after you
      3. whites are racist
      4. all whites have money
      5. whites have had it easier than Blacks

CHAPTER THREE: PRESEASON CONDITIONING   **27**

CHAPTER FOUR: GATHERING THE EQUIPMENT 55

CHAPTER FIVE:
THE MARATHON BEGINS   103

CHAPTER SIX: CROSSING THE FINISH LINE A WINNER   **139**

     A. What Type of Test?
     B. Spread Exam Preparation Time
     C. Gather Your Sources
     D. Gather Possible Questions
     E. Review Outline
     F. Pretest Yourself
     G. Check
     H. Review Outline
     I. Lock in Using Memory System
     J. Test Yourself
     K Review Outline
     L. Final Test
     M. Cool Out
     N. If Cramming Is Necessary...

I.   Why You Should Prepare to Cheat on an Exam   143

II. Test Taking: How to Come Through In the Clutch   144
     A. Don't Forget Your Name
     B. Relax
     C. Read the Directions
     D. Read the Whole Exam
     E. Let Your Mind Go
         1. scribble immediate ideas
         2. scribble formulas/factors/ingredients
     F. Answer, Easiest to More Difficult
     G. True-False
     H. Multiple choice

     I. Essay:
         1. scan all questions: short or long answers?
         2. look at the call
         3. go for what you know
         4. outline it first

CHAPTER ONE

"FREE YOUR MIND, AND YOUR ASS WILL FOLLOW..."

"Liberty is not merely a privilege to be conferred; it is a habit to be acquired."

Lloyd George

"Free your mind and your ass will follow, for the kingdom of heaven is within..."

George Clinton, Parliament/Funkadelic

SURVIVAL

Survival is the overwhelming constant during the African's long and painful sojourn through the fog of world history. Despite repeated attempts at cultural eradication, genocide, and economic, physical and mental slavery, we have survived, and, to a degree, thrived here on these American shores distant from our original homelands.

WHAT THIS BOOK IS DESIGNED TO DO

I have condensed some of the lessons learned from the personal experiences of Black students, including myself, who have been where you are going. Every fact, hint or technique is the result of experience, observation, empirical research, or the hindsight of students who have made mistakes you don't have to make. This book is not a work of fiction, nor a jokebook.

The experiences and observations are largely related to my attendance, as well as the attendance of other Black students, at a large, predominantly white state university, the University of Florida. However, the techniques for success and the obstacles one encounters are basically the same, no matter what type of school you attend; high school, college, or graduate or professional school. If you use this book as a guide, your grades, attitude, and self-confidence will improve.

I do not pull punches and I do not mince words. The opinions expressed are mine alone. Therefore, some may attack this book as racist, paranoid, unrealistic. Some of my colleagues, former instructors, and friends may be hurt by the strong opinions expressed here.

So be it. The situations are real and they are true. This book is written from the perspective of a Black student to Black students. I ask you to use what you can of the ideas, techniques and opinions presented, find a system that works for you, and throw the rest away.

I am convinced, through personal experience, observation, and study, that there is a thick veneer of racism in American higher education that reflects the attitudes and actions of the larger society. Let this book serve as your warning and preparation for the 'brave new world' of opportunity and responsibility which racial integration has wrought.

LIFE AT THE ACADEMIC "BIG HOUSE"

Students in major colleges and universities are like the house and field slaves in giant plantations. We have little control over our lives. We are usually dependent on the college or university to provide food, clothing and shelter through financial aid; Black students in particular are made to feel like 'welfare queens' for accepting financial aid, particularly minority scholarships, or any other help primarily used by 'minorities.'

Black students are considered by many to be intellectually inferior, a 'disadvantaged' group who are being educated (civilized?) through the beneficence of a system which is attempting to rescue us from our own savagery.

But as in slavery, a contest of minds and wills is being played. And just as some slaves were able to outwit 'Ol Massa' at his own game, you too can win! The key is in harnessing both your spiritual power and the power of your own mind.

MY STORY

I have always been pretty happy-go-lucky regarding school. I have always done well, even though I never liked school that much. I got out of high school and college with B+ averages in each; I partied, hung out, and had a great time in each. I was on the track and basketball teams in high school. I ran track and played intramural basketball in college, and was always pretty popular.

I entered law school at the University of Florida, Gainesville, Florida (UF), 'on a humbug'. My Law School Aptitude Test (LSAT) scores were substantially above the average for Black students, and slightly above the average for white students. Good LSAT scores were critical to admission to any American law school.

My grades and test scores were high enough to get me admitted to UF's College of Law under their Affirmative Action program. After graduation from college, I was unable to convince my employer, an Atlanta television station, to hire me full time for more than minimum wage. Off to law school I went.

During my first year in law school (1978-79), I had heard that the University was offering a joint Juris Doctor/Master of Business Administration (JD/MBA) degree, with $3000 per year in scholarship grant money. (This was a lot of money in those days.) Since I was using loans to go to law school, I thought I could get into the MBA program and help pay for the law school education, and not be in so much debt after graduation.

I didn't know what I was doing.

I was a journalism major in college, and had never taken a business class during either high school or college; had taken no Accounting, no Statistics, no Finance, no Management or Computer courses. When I was accepted in the business school, I had not taken a math class in five years. I had never seen a financial statement; I didn't know the difference between a debit and a credit; didn't know how to balance a checkbook.

For the next three and one-half years, I competed against students who graduated from colleges with high honors in Accounting, Computer Science, Engineering, Statistics, Finance, and Business Administration. I took the same classes they did: Quantitative Analysis, Cost Accounting, Corporate Finance, etc. A 3.0 cumulative grade point (a B average), was required for graduation.

At the same time, I was taking courses at the College of Law, and was dangerously close to flunking out after my first year, since I made mostly C's. The law school required a C average to graduate.

For the first time, I saw myself in trouble academically.

For the first time, I had to get serious in school.

It almost killed me.

WHAT I DID

The first thing that I did was to set what I believed to be realistic goals about my level of performance.

I made a calculated decision that, at the graduate and professional levels, I preferred graduation to high grades. At that time, I was unwilling to pay the price, to go the extra mile that it sometimes takes to achieve excellence.

Thus, my goal in law school and business school was not to make A's; not to make the Dean's List, the Honor Roll, Law Review, the scholastic honorary societies. My goal in law school was to get a C average and get the hell out, pass the bar exam, and attempt to live life as a normal human being. My goal in business school was to get a B average, graduate, and go down life's merry road to forge my destiny, two diplomas in hand.

My goal, like the goal of so many other Black students, was SUR-VIVAL. ·

Some readers may say "Well, Cherry, aren't you saying it's OK to be mediocre? Aren't you telling Black students that it's OK not to do your best?"

No. That is not what I'm saying.

I was not a perfect student. In retrospect, the key mistake that I made was in not calculating the extra effort that it would take to achieve academic excellence.

What I have discovered since is this: THE ROAD FROM ACADEMIC MEDIOCRITY TO ACADEMIC EXCELLENCE IS ALWAYS SHORTER THAN YOU THINK.

I could have made better grades by doing only a little bit more work than I did. But the techniques that I put together during my graduate education were so powerful that I was still able to accomplish my goal, which was to be awarded two graduate degrees simultaneously.

At the same time, I knew that school served a social function. I knew that a lot of action occurs outside of class in interactions with students. I knew that I would remember the lifelong friends I made, the social events I attended, and the strange incidents that happened in my academic career much longer than I would remember those valuable nuggets of knowledge that dropped from instructor's mouths.

Basically, I wanted to party and still pass my classes, and I did. I graduated the same day from two academically challenging programs, as one of a handful of students in the history of the University to ever do so. It was an indescribable feeling leaving one graduation ceremony, Juris Doctor in hand, to another to pick up a Master of Business Administration degree, after four and one-half years of joy and pain, work, and anxiety.

The system I used allowed me to party, hang out, travel, goof off, and generally have a great time despite the intensity and academic pressure of competing for grades in two rigorous graduate-level programs. If it can work for me, considering my woeful academic preparation for the ordeal I found myself in, it can certainly get you A's in middle school, high school or college.

The individual goals that you set are up to you. But I believe that <u>EVERY</u> high school or college student should, as a rule, set graduation with a B average as a minimum goal, regardless of the major. By setting anything less, you are seriously hurting your chances to land either an entry-level job of your choice, or progressing to the undergrad, grad or professional school of your choice.

WHY RE-INVENT THE WHEEL?

Most folks I know don't want to work any harder than they have to accomplish a particular goal. I'm no different.

King Solomon, the well-known Biblical wise man, once said that there is nothing new under the sun. This can be easily applied to academics and the skills needed to be successful.

Therefore, it made no sense for me to re-invent the wheel and develop a system of studying heretofore unknown to modern man. All I did while I was in school was find out what systems existed, pick out a few, and tinker with them until I found out what worked for me.

For memory, I relied on a memory expert, Harry Lorayne. For making study outlines, I noticed how commercial law school course outlines were put together. For essay tests, I looked at model answers. For multiple choice (which I will abbreviate in this book as 'multichoice' tests), I got info from multichoice exam review material. For speed reading, I took a professional course. For note-taking, I went to the library and studied books on how to take notes.

One thing before I go further: Don't get the idea that you are gonna use this book to bluff your way in and out, scheming on everybody along the way. This book will not help you if you are not willing to work, work and work some more. It will not help you if you do not have discipline or are unwilling to develop it. If you fall into either of these categories, you are wasting your time. Give this book to somebody who is serious about school.

NAME YOUR WEAPON

By nature, I am a rebel, like almost everyone.

I like to think that if I were a slave some 150 years ago in this country, I would have been the kind who may have been beaten to death for attacking Ol' Massa in broad daylight with a butcher knife. Or maybe I would have been a house slave trying to pick the right opportunity to poison Ol' Massa when he wasn't watching. (Actually, I probably would have been too paralyzed by fear and terror, like most other slaves, to do anything.)

I am always looking for an edge, for a different way to accomplish a goal, without losing my personal dignity and without fitting into somebody else's mold. If you were a slave, and if your goal was freedom, you could do it one of two ways: big and bold and maybe get beaten to death, or you could do it by a tactic we can call 'misdirection'.

Most slaves were masters (forgive the pun) at misdirection, which is the art of making somebody focus on one thing while you are doing another. The 'happy' slaves singing all those mournful songs that even Ol' Massa grew to love were actually coded messages to runaway slaves and others on the probabilities of successful escapes. What Ol' Massa focused on was what he thought was real; the truth was quite different.

Contrast the strategies of John Brown and Harriet Tubman during the slave era.

Brown thought of himself as the avenging hand of God, and attempted to start a violent slave rebellion by murdering white folks in their homes, and gathering an army of slaves along the way. Freedom or death. Brown and his army ended up getting shot, burned, or hung, though Brown himself became a martyr for the cause of abolition.

Tubman took the opposite approach. After establishing a series of secret 'stations' on the Underground Railway running south to north, she figuratively 'stole' slaves from the plantations at night, one at a time, under cover of darkness. Those old slave songs, part of a strategy of stealth and misdirection, were critical factors in the success of the Underground Railway. Note that the Underground Railway's success was also due, in large part, to the participation of sympathetic whites who were opponents of slavery.

NOW YOU SEE ME...

I decided early in the game not to take the John Brown approach and become a martyr for the academic cause. My personal strategy of higher education was based on misdirection. I always wanted instructors, classmates, and others to see and focus on one part of me or my personality while I was doing something else. Essentially, I played on the knowledge that many white folks, particularly those in power, will consistently underestimate the capabilities of Blacks until they are shown different. And even then a lot of them may think a Black person who succeeds is a fluke.

That crucial miscalculation, underestimation and low expectations of the Black student's motivation and capabilities, was my edge. It can be almost every Black student's edge.

Ah, I see that I now have your attention.

Read on ...

CHAPTER TWO

ATTITUDE ADJUSTMENT

There is little hope for us until we become tough-minded enough to break loose from the shackles of prejudice, half-truths, and downright ignorance.

— Martin Luther King, Jr.

YOUR BLACKNESS: HANDICAP OR HELP ?

Yep. Right off the bat, race rears its ugly head.

The following list is a few generalizations of how whites and Blacks feel about each other. They are not listed because they are true; they are listed because many people believe them and because they may crucially affect your academic environment.

COMMON ASSUMPTIONS BLACKS MAKE ABOUT WHITES

1. Whites are smarter than Blacks. Whites always know what they are doing. This attitude is very prevalent among Black people world-wide from South Africa to South Carolina.

How did this message become prevalent?

Every second, every day, for more than 600 years, since the first European explorer set foot on the continent of Africa, the message to anyone 'unfortunate' enough to be born with Black skin has always been the same: OUR WHITE SKIN IS SUPERIOR. OUR WHITE

CULTURE IS ADVANCED AND SUPERIOR. YOUR BLACK SKIN IS INFERIOR. YOUR BLACK CULTURE IS PRIMITIVE AND INFERIOR. IT IS NATURAL AND CORRECT FOR US TO CONTROL. IT IS NATURAL AND CORRECT FOR YOU TO SERVE.

Why did this message become prevalent?

In a nutshell, it was a critical factor in justifying, in white folks' minds, the wholesale destruction of the continent of Africa during the years of active slave trading (from approximately 1400 until the 1860's). By then, this message had become so entrenched world-wide, that it is virtually considered a law of nature even to this day. In my opinion, the idea of white superiority (and its close cousin, American superiority) are the real reasons for this country's occasionally arrogant intervention into everybody else's affairs.

You see the same kind of attitude at work these days when many prominent university and college officials complain about the 'compromise of academic standards' and the 'decline of the quality of scholastic research' as a consequence of affirmative action and the arrival of Black students and faculty on white campuses.

I'm sure, in your life experiences, you have had the chance to meet quite a few dumb, stupid white folks, just as you have had the chance to meet some dumb, stupid Black folks. If not, you can look at America today and see what 'smart' white people who run the country have done: a single bank bankrolling international dope dealers and known terrorists with the cooperation of the U.S. government; people losing their life's savings in savings and loans, insurance companies, and stock market scams. Crime, dishonesty, poverty, disrespect for humanity, and the mad dash for the dollar here in the land of opportunity.

So as far as white superiority is concerned, don't believe the hype.

2. White people are after you. Most don't even know you exist and don't care. Some who know you exist don't think you are important enough to be concerned about. However, some may be concerned about you for various reasons, including their own insecurities about

their own academic capabilities. Some folks consider you a threat to their own grades, and resent your presence in 'their' school. Just because you may be paranoid doesn't mean somebody's not following you. However, that somebody may be Black. One never knows, does one?

3. <u>Whites are racist.</u> Some are and some aren't. I heard a sister named Patricia Russell-McCloud give a speech. Something she said struck a responsive chord in me. She said, "Some people are of your kind and not of your color; other people are of your color but are not of your kind."

If you fall into the trap of condemning all people not of your color, you are twice victimized: once by a system that fosters racist, superior attitudes toward those who are different; and once by yourself, by refusing to rise above the evil that surrounds you. The latter situation is worse because you have imprisoned yourself in a cell made with your own hands.

4. <u>All whites have money.</u> Many do but most don't. Note, however, that Blacks and whites have different scales of wealth. For instance, a Black family in which both parents are employed as teachers would probably be considered an upper-middle income family by other Blacks. However, a white couple who are both teachers would probably be considered lower middle class by whites.

The key, I believe, is in each race's financial expectations and levels of financial satisfaction within each particular group. Black folks in America have been so poor for so long that when we get a little money in our pockets, we get satisfied. And since we never made any real money before, our expectations of ever getting any are much lower than that of our white counterparts.

What does this have to do with academic survival? Well, an obsession with other folks' financial condition could lead to attitude problems in you: resentment, self-condemnation, lack of self-confidence, lowered self-esteem. This can lead to a sense of hopelessness and defeatism that takes you out of the game before you even start. It can also lead to vicious hatred against all white folks that vents itself violently or criminally.

Some Black folks steal, kill and pillage because of an attitude problem that THEY have about themselves and about white folks that is based upon a lie. If you are one of them, you need to check yourself.

5. <u>Whites have had it easier than Blacks.</u> Some have and some haven't. There are some white folks I wouldn't dream of trading places with; the Massachusetts Kennedys, for example. Keep the money and the fame. I'll take my normal, somewhat anonymous childhood and my Mom and Dad who are still alive and well, at this writing.

The most insidious thing about this particular myth is that it may make you believe that white folks owe you something. Look, nobody owes you anything.

Yeah, I know we've been 'buked and we been scorned in this country for more than 400 years. I know we've worked sunup to sundown, chopping that cotton, totin' that barge and liftin' that bale, and still ain't got a paycheck for it. I KNOW that.

But if the American government hasn't paid us for 400 years of free work, what makes you think an instructor, particularly a white instructor, is gonna give you a B instead of a C in the 1990s? Get real!

Hey, I'm no fool. Nobody in his right mind would say that whites generally haven't had better opportunities to succeed in America than Blacks, especially since white folks, including non-American white folks, own most of the assets of this country. Still, most whites haven't really succeeded like they always thought they would. Some have not been successful because of the same problems that affect us: lack of self-confidence, low motivation, etc. Greater opportunity does not guarantee success.

COMMON ASSUMPTIONS WHITES MAKE ABOUT BLACKS

1. <u>Blacks are intellectually inferior to whites.</u> I firmly believe that this is the most important misapprehension that whites, and unfortunately, many Blacks, have about Black people.

However, this particular myth is potentially the most important weapon in your arsenal in the psychological battles that are constantly fought among Black students, white students, and instructors. Note, however, that this is true ONLY IF YOU DO NOT BELIEVE THIS MYTH YOURSELF.

If you DO believe that Blacks are intellectually inferior, you have problems to be solved that are beyond the scope of this book. However, reading some of the books listed in the List of References and Appendix may give you a good start in debunking this myth.

AN HISTORICAL EXPLANATION OF THIS IMPORTANT ASSUMPTION

There have been two fairly recent major theories that have been advanced by American social science to explain the 'fact' that Blacks are intellectually inferior to whites.

The first theory says we are inferior because we are born that way (i.e. genetic reasons); the second theory says we are inferior because of our inferior culture and environment (i.e. cultural deprivation). Both of these theories have enjoyed cycles of popularity here in America in attempting to explain what is the real deal with 'America's underprivileged minority'.

Since the beginning of the 20th century, one American psychologist after another has come up with some study giving credence to the belief that Blacks are genetically inferior, even to the present day. However, the genetic theory became less popular in the public politically liberal days of the John F. Kennedy and Lyndon Johnson presidential administrations of the 1960's.

At that time, the cultural deprivation theory took hold and became popularized by Daniel Moynihan's 1965 report that blamed Black America's problems on family instability rather than racism. The Moynihan report laid the foundation for the belief that the Black community, particularly the Black family, cannot provide the proper environment and background for the success of its children.

It was a case of America stabbing Blacks in the back and calling it suicide. When in doubt, blame the victim.

The Moynihan report was like bread from heaven to a starving American moral conscience. The American government decided compensatory education was the key to addressing the academic problems of Black children. Note that the 'compensation' was for the poor Black child who was deprived of the predominantly Eurocentric American culture that his young white counterpart enjoyed at home daily.

Thus, Black youngsters were head started, upward bounded, remediated, enriched, and affirmatively actioned from the late 60's to the late 70's. Some programs, such as Head Start, <u>have</u> been highly effective in accomplishing its desired goal. Almost all others have been marginally successful, or have been total shams on the public. Note again that almost none of these programs were conceived, originated, organized, initiated, or managed by the very people they were designed to serve.

In the late '70s and early '80s, American social scientists again went to work, analyzing the data about the effectiveness of compensatory education. According to their measurements, it was a failure. Standardized test scores were still low, as were reading levels. Dropout rates and unemployment were still high.

As a consequence of the perceived failure of compensatory education, the pendulum swung back toward the genetic theory of inferiority. It was as if America was saying, "We have tried to help them to the best of our ability; we have spent billions on government programs. Maybe Black people are just naturally dumber than we are."

And if you don't think that people around the world believe that, just read any current magazine or your local newspaper. In 1986, Japan's Prime Minister Yashuhiro Nakasone said that the real reason America lagged behind Japan in technology was because of the large U.S. population of Blacks and Hispanics whose low intelligence levels are holding the country back. In 1990, Nakasone's successor, Prime Minister Toshiki Taifu, claimed that Blacks affected America like pimps and prostitutes affect a decent neighborhood: they destroy the worth of the local community.

I believe many Americans, of all races, deep in their spirits, agree with this statement even to this day.

HOW STANDARDIZED TESTING AND TEACHER EXPECTATION AFFECT THE ASSUMPTION OF BLACK INFERIORITY

Standardized testing and teacher expectation are two other factors that are also crucial in buttressing the widespread myth of Black academic inferiority.

Standardized Testing: Again, a short historical summary is in order.

A Frenchman by the name of Alfred Binet, in the early 1900's, laid the foundation for what we now call 'standardized testing', which includes the intelligence quotient (IQ) tests, the Scholastic Aptitude Test (SAT), and others like them.

Binet had been hired by the French government to help solve the problem of student placement in French schools, which were extremely overcrowded. One solution was to separate the slower students from the better students, since the slower students were holding up progress.

Binet then developed a test that could separate students according to their academic readiness, the scholastic sheep from the goats, so to speak. The original IQ test that he and his associate Theodore Simon conceived tested students on many things they had learned in class. In order for a question to be used on the Binet-Simon test, a large percentage of the smarter French students had to be able to answer it correctly. It was these students who set the standard for the others.

Binet's test became popular with American social scientists. The Americans gave it a very convenient scoring system, in which an IQ score of 100 was considered average, scores under 85 were considered borderline retarded, and 115 and above was considered above average. In order for a question to be used on the American IQ test, a large percentage of American-born WHITE children, from a sample of children chosen by the American scientists, had to answer the question correctly. It was this group of children who set the standard for all others who subsequently took the test.

Therein lies part of the problem for the Black student. We are beat up side the head every day with the fact that Blacks' standardized test scores of all kinds are way below our white counterparts. Under the circumstances, they should be because the questions don't ask us things within our cultural experience, and maybe not within our educational experience.

The other part of the problem is the fact that Binet never meant IQ scores to be used as some fixed, unchangeable, God-given absolute measure of one person's intelligence. It was only to be used to determine which child may need special tutoring because he or she was deficient in a particular academic area.

America has gone test-crazy. To drive a bus, you gotta take a psychological profile test. Tests to get in school; tests to get out. Many tests have 'nothing to do with nothing', so to speak.

The tragic thing is that these bogus standardized test scores are like giant millstones around the Black student's neck. Joseph L. White, in his book The Psychology of Blacks: An Afro-American Perspective (Prentice-Hall, Englewood Cliffs, NJ: 1984) describes the academic conspiracy this way:

> The most able American schoolchildren could be
> identified early and given the kind of education nec-
> essary to develop their superior talents. Intellectually
> talented children identified by the IQ test would be
> groomed as future leaders of America-a sort of
> power elite built on mental giftedness...Less talented
> children would be conditioned by teaching methods
> focusing on drill, rote memory, order, punctuality,
> and obedience to prepare them to fit easily into the
> lock-step routine of America's factories where they

would work as adults....Those with IQs of 140 and
above were not only thought to have superior intellectual endowment, but were also considered to be
of superior moral character. To put it bluntly, they
were just better human beings than those with
average and below average IQs.

(at page 107)

Numerous recent studies have shown that IQ tests tend to favor
those with backgrounds similar to middle-class white children and
that IQ scores can be improved with experience. But meantime,
thousands of Black children have been classified as retarded, devel-
opmentally handicapped, or shuffled off to so-called 'special education' classes as a result of poor test scores.

Teacher Expectations: From first grade, your school system has
kept a file on you, usually called a cumulative record. This record will
follow you for the rest of your academic career.

Your record includes test scores, grades, and previous teacher
evaluations of you. Because your record goes where you go, it can
give a teacher who reads it a broad picture of what academic performance to expect from you.

Additionally, teachers bring their own socialization and life experiences in setting expectations of students. Again, White puts it suc-
cinctly:

Opinions (about students)... are also influenced by
race and socioeconomic level. If a student has a low
IQ, is Black and is from a low socioeconomic group,
he or she is more likely to be viewed as not having a
high probability of achieving classroom success,
especially by white teachers. Once established,
expectations are resistant to change. Teachers tend
to spend much less time in positive classroom contact with students whom they expect to be poor
learners... Teachers seem to invest a greater amount
of positive effort in the high IQ-economically advan-
taged student, effort expressed in more frequent

praise, attention, affectionate gestures, and assignments to classroom leadership roles.

(at page 115)

Various studies conclude that a teacher's expectations of how
well (or poorly) a student will perform is of critical importance in the
student's ability to perform well.

White also points out two social/cultural/historical factors that prevent white teachers from having the high expectations of Black students that could propel the student to higher academic achievement:

1. <u>Inherent racism in the American society.</u> Because of the day-in,
day-out image of Blacks as 'mentally inferior sambos, clowns, noble
savages and beasts', according to White, most whites are overtly or
subtly tainted by attitudes of cultural, racial, and intellectual superiority. Thus, teachers are unable to perceive the true intellectual strength
of the Black student, and are unable to relate to or motivate the
Black student.

Says White:

> Many humanitarian liberal white teachers, those who
> love and want to save all poor Black folks, attempt to
> shield Black students from failure by operating with a
> permanent set of lowered expectations. Shielding
> Black students from failure by imposing a permanent
> set of lowered expectations is only another way of
> communicating to them that they are not capable
> of achieving. (at 117)

2. <u>Black students may not fit a white teacher's mold of how a
good student walks, talks, and acts.</u> A number of studies show
marked differences in how Black teachers and white teachers perceive the Black student. The white teachers saw the Black students in
the study as high-strung, lazy, rebellious, and talkative; Black teachers
saw them as energetic, cooperative, ambitious, and happy. Do you
think that these two wildly different evaluations will have an effect on
the teachers' expectations?

In the Introduction to this book, I wrote about a strategy called <u>misdirection</u> that depended on underestimation of a Black student's motivation and intellectual capabilities. The assumption that Blacks are intellectually inferior to whites is the key to the misdirection strategy.

Think of it this way. Suppose Congress made a law that every household in the U.S. had to take in at least one chimpanzee (i.e. a monkey) a year and train it because chimps had become an endangered species. But you're not Michael Jackson; you don't want a chimp; you don't like chimps. You would rather have a cocker spaniel.

But, you are a law-abiding citizen and when the government delivers your chimp, you take it despite the fact that you are highly upset about this law.

By some bureaucratic miracle of governmental selection, suppose that one year they gave you a chimp who could discuss the theory of evolution vs. creationism with you over a cup of coffee at the breakfast table. This would blow you away because all your experience had taught you that chimps are of limited intelligence (and that they don't drink coffee).

Your natural tendency would be to take good care of that chimp because of its special talents. You may even learn to love that chimp. But would you change your belief that chimps are generally of limited intelligence? No. Deep in your heart, you would believe that no matter how smart that chimp is, he would never be as smart as you. So you may even try to teach the chimp more to find out the limits of his capabilities.

Without a doubt, you would believe that your chimp is the <u>exception to the general rule.</u> The only way you would change your opinion would be to become knowledgeable about chimps, maybe through personal contact, study, etc. But unless you saw a fairly large number of chimps who had the same kind of intelligence yours did, you would believe that all chimps are poor dumb animals.

In my opinion, America still perceives Black folks largely as chimps, even in the 1990s. The sad thing is that many Black folks believe the same thing about themselves. Look at the ingrained images of us that have been burned into the societal consciousness over time: pimps, thieves, a lazy and shiftless people, a bunch of crybabies always looking for a handout, either angry and sullen or happy go lucky. Maybe not really dumb, but certainly slower than average.

I believe that modern American racism and prejudice takes more of a turn toward cultural and intellectual arrogance these days, rather than toward the boldness of the physical confrontation of years past. But if you are shrewd, you can still take advantage of a bad situation.

I'll briefly use the chimp example to introduce you to another crucial factor in the academic environment: AFFIRMATIVE ACTION.

Just as you didn't want your government-mandated chimp, you can be sure that the major white institutions, by and large, didn't want to participate in affirmative action programs.

Affirmative action is a wicked double-edged sword that cuts both Black student and white institution to the bone. The institutions hate it because it brings to light the fraud of equal educational opportunity that continues to be perpetrated on American society, Blacks in particular. They also hate it because it has been crammed down their collective organizational throats beginning in the 1970s as the result of numerous court orders, settlements, and judgments.

I believe this extreme distaste for affirmative action has a 'trickle-down' effect from the school administration, to the department heads, to the faculty, to the classroom, and finally in the Black student-to-teacher relationship. It particularly manifests itself in lower expectations of Black students, resulting in a condescending attitude on behalf of the instructor toward the Black student. You can witness the same phenomenon in the American corporate business community, which has discovered the word "quota", and has successfully used the lie of reverse discrimination to avoid dealing with the fact of continuing, provable discrimination in American business.

I have seen affirmative action make and break Black students.

It helped me get into grad school. My law school test scores were not high enough to be admitted as a 'regular' student. I say <u>helped</u> deliberately, because it was my willingness to work, sweat, scheme, and study, along with the grace of God, that got me out of grad school with two diplomas.

It broke other students who believed that because they were admitted under affirmative action guidelines, they were less than qualified to attend school. It was a psychological burden that eventually wore them down.

I'll never forget the day in my first-year Constitutional Law class where a white student said that if she was admitted to school via an affirmative action program, she would feel embarrassed and ashamed because it would prove that she wasn't as good as everybody else. Every black hand in that classroom wanted to wrap itself around that woman's throat.

The tragedy is that I personally know Black students who believe that what that woman said in class was, and is, true.

But the beautiful thing about the whole affirmative action dilemma is that when you become the <u>exception to the rule,</u> the instructors can't handle it. When you seem to be working hard; when you are competitive with the rest of the class grade-wise; when you are going the extra mile to do the small things that make you stand out above the crowd, the instructors will respond. Not necessarily because they care about you, though some will.

Some will respond, and sometimes go overboard for you, because <u>they never thought you could do it.</u> For them, you have become the <u>exception</u>, the oddity, the curiosity. Sort of like the Elephant Man in the circus.

You have <u>misdirected</u> them by using their own racist assumption against them, by having them focus on your differences from what they believe is normal behavior for a Black student. But you know in your heart that there are millions of brothers and sisters who have the same intelligence, the same drive, the same motivation as you, but who just have not had the chance to 'get in the race'.

You do know that, don't you?

Again, the key to the misdirection strategy is <u>to make yourself seem the exception to the general rule of Black academic inferiority.</u> By the end of this book, you will know how to do that. Meanwhile, back to our common assumptions.

2. <u>All Blacks have some type of artistic or athletic talent.</u> Wrong. I'm a personal testimony to that. I can't draw a straight line with a ruler. I can't sing a note. I can't tie shoelaces without written instructions (just kidding on that one). But what does this have to do with studying and academic survival? Stay tuned.

3. <u>Blacks are economically and culturally deprived.</u> This may be true in many whites' eyes. If so, then it may be because their standards are different, but not necessarily better. If a man has enough to eat everyday and can provide the basic necessities so that his family can live in relative comfort, safety, and dignity, who's to say that he is poor? Where there is love, there is an abundance of riches greater than gold.

Because most Blacks have no way of tracing our ancestry more than three or four generations, does that mean we are culturally poor? Of course not. In fact we are a tri-cultural people. We still enjoy remnants of our native African culture. We developed a different culture by necessity, separate and apart from American culture, during slavery. Now we are slowly taking on aspects of the larger American cultures and mores as a result of integration. Our people are culturally rich, but ignorant of our history.

WHY IS THIS STUFF IMPORTANT?

The goal of this chapter is to give you a starting point, an idea of the probable mindsets of some of the participants in the academic marathon. Those participants are you, your classmates, your instructors, and the institution itself.

Evaluate your own mindset first. Do you feel that somebody is after you because of the color of your skin? If you do, does this feeling prevent you from studying and going about your everyday activities effectively? I hope not. A careful person is aware of the people around him and takes the proper precautions to protect himself physically, mentally, spiritually and emotionally from his enemies-both seen and unseen.

Do you truly feel that Blacks are inferior in everything but athletics and entertainment? Do you feel that we have no culture or history of our own? If so, I refer you to some of the books on Black history listed in the List of References and Appendix of this book.

Now examine the attitudes of your Black classmates (if you have any). You are important to each other because you can be of mutual comfort and support in the hard times that will come.

Do any of them exhibit a hang-dog look which <u>may</u> indicate a negative, defeatist attitude? (I say <u>may</u> because some people have a natural hang-dog look.)

If their attitude is negative, dig into your jeans pocket and buy them a copy of this book. After you do that and they still give you the finger, don't try to convert them. Stay away from them. Anybody that has a negative attitude about school or about themselves is poison to you. You've sown the seed; maybe it will sprout later. Leave it alone and work the strategies in this book to the best of your ability.

If you happen to find other Black students on the same wavelength as you, it should be easy to establish a rapport with them. But for goodness sakes, BE YOURSELF! DON'T get friendly with somebody just to use him or her later. School is a place where lifelong relationships are, and should be, developed. Take advantage of the opportunity to make and become a true friend.

Evaluate the attitudes of your white classmates. Remember, somebody not of your color may be of your kind. Interact with them on the level which you feel most comfortable: athletic, social, organizational, classroom, etc. Pay attention to your gut instincts-your 'vibrations', about people. (I know this sounds sort of spooky.)

Try to identify why you feel as you do. Are you picking up 'vibes' of jealousy, fear, discomfort, curiosity, envy, respect, etc.? Pay attention to these feelings, try to classify them, then put them in the back of your mind for future reference. There is no need to keep a 'book' on your classmates because it's a waste of time. They will only affect your strategy a little anyway.

The other important 'attitude evaluation' will be that of the instructors. This is a little more difficult because most students have limited contact with instructors outside of class. So all you have to go on are observations; yours, fellow students and former students. This process is also called 'getting the scoop' on the instructors.

Feel your instructors and classmates out. Are they exhibiting signs of intellectual arrogance? Do they answer questions that are asked, or do they respond in ways that attempt to impress you with their knowledge? Is your instructor's reaction to your questions different from reactions to questions from your white classmates? Ask other Black students in the class (if there are any) to observe. We will get into more detail on this in the section on manipulating instructors.

Again, pay close attention to your gut instinct about the teacher. What kind of vibes do you pick up? Can you classify these vibes? How do you personally feel about the instructor? What was your first impression of him or her?

Note, however, that vibes are NOT the determining factor in making up your mind about an instructor. Vibes are only one factor; later, you can look at old tests, classroom notes, the instructor's teaching style, and your personal contact with him and use all those factors and others in mapping out your strategy to make the best grade.

SUMMARY

WHITE PEOPLE GENERALLY, AND WHITE STUDENTS PARTICULARLY, ARE NOT SMARTER BECAUSE OF THE COLOR OF THEIR SKIN.

Standardized test scores have been misused by the American academic institution, and society generally, and have been used consciously and subconsciously to justify the myth of Black academic inferiority.

It is a proven fact that teacher expectations can affect academic performance. Generally, white teachers have lowered expectations of Black students. This can work in your favor if you can position yourself as the exception to this academic 'rule' of Black academic inferiority.

CHAPTER THREE

PRESEASON CONDITIONING

Do you not know that in a race, all the runners run,
but one gets the prize? Run in such a way as to get
the prize. Everyone who competes in the game goes
into strict training...I do not run like a man running
aimlessly, I do not fight like a man beating the air...

1 Corinthians 9: 24,26 (The Bible,
New International Version)

No athlete in his right mind would compete in a major athletic
competition without preparing his body and mind for the rigors of the
contest before game day. Can you imagine being at the starting line
at the Olympic marathon, knowing that you have not run a single
mile in practice? Believe me, you'll get the same feeling just before
your instructor hands you your test paper of a crucial exam, and you
know you don't know anything about the subject tested. Just as the
Olympic marathoner must train long before he gets to that starting
line, so must you prepare and train before that quiz, midterm, or final
exam is placed on your desk.

PREPARING THE MIND

GAINING SELF-CONFIDENCE

Your mind is really the only natural weapon you have to win the athletic competition. Yet by various estimates, human beings only use a fraction of potential 'brain power' that the good Lord gave us. The key is to maximize your use of your natural thinking abilities.

As a student, you have only a moderate amount of control over your life. You go to class when told, sleep where you're assigned, eat what the cafeteria offers. You play when you can. Your worth as a student, and sometimes as a human being, is judged by a stranger who doesn't know you and probably never met you. Just about all the events that happen in your academic life are beyond your control.

It is this feeling of powerlessness and lack of control in a pressurized, grade-conscious, competitively cutthroat environment that literally drives students crazy and sometimes to suicide. Almost all major colleges and universities in this country have full-time psychological counseling services, and they are there for a reason. For instance, at finals time, students are lined up around the block for help.

If you are to cope, you must realize that you can't control everything in your life. A cynic would say that belief in God or some 'force' allows you to rationalize to yourself the reason why you seem to do everything right and still get screwed.

The bottom line is that even if you follow all the instructions in this book; even if you read every book ever written on how to study; there will still be occasions when things will go wrong. Do you fold up your tent and pack it in? No! You've only suffered a temporary setback.

Whether you believe in God or not, if you have thoroughly examined the situation and truly believe in your heart you've done all you can, DON'T BLAME YOURSELF! Consistency and perseverance will pay off for you in time.

WHY BLACK STUDENTS SHOULD HAVE SELF-CONFIDENCE

I firmly believe that many of the problems Black students have, especially in the predominately white institutions, are due primarily to a lack of self-confidence. This is caused both by the collective and wholesale brainwashing of Blacks over hundreds of years as well as by the subliminal 'mental massage' of today's contemporary American society which continues to reinforce the stereotypic image of the intellectually inferior/athletically superior Black race. Black students are literally dying mentally and academically for lack of knowledge of their own past.

A SIDE TRIP INTO HISTORY

It is important to know that you are part of a whole, proud, strong, intelligent people with a long and noble, yet tragic, heritage. Because of a warped, demonic biological selection system as a consequence of slavery, we are descendants of the best human specimens Africa had to offer the world. We are the survivors of the fittest, physically and emotionally. Even with all our problems, no other race of people (except our brothers and sisters still in Africa) have had to walk the road we have. Yet we have survived and will thrive here in America. This is what I call your sociological point of reference.

These days almost every individual claims that he or she is a 'survivor'. Well, I'm here to tell you that no group of individuals has survived like Black Americans.

First, contrary to popular belief, we are an ancient people.

Whether you believe in Biblical creationism or the theory of evolution, it is an uncontroverted fact that the African continent is the cradle of world civilization.

Understand one thing: if you are Black, you are African. It matters not if you prefer to call yourself Jamaican, Haitian, Bahamian, Cuban, a New Yorker, or whatever. All that means is that your ancestors probably got off the slave ship a little earlier (or later) than mine did, or at a different place from my ancestors.

African civilizations housed the world's first and greatest centers of learning in Timbuktu; formed the first democratic governments; built the pyramids; were the chosen people of God who miraculously crossed the Red Sea with Moses; conceived the first idea of monotheism, i.e. belief in One God, rather than the many gods, as the Greeks and Romans believed.

The remarkable thing about these accomplishments is that they were done in spite of environmental and social conditions that would have killed off a weaker people. And they were done thousands of years ago, under the worst conditions possible.

The long tradition of African achievement continued, even after our wholesale enslavement and export to America.

The first man to die for this country was Crispus Attucks, a Black man. He was killed by the British just before the Revolutionary War. Even before the war, Black fighting men had developed a tradition of service in the military, having fought wars against the French and (unfortunately) the Native Americans.

Only in the last 20 years or so have conditions truly begun to improve for Black America. But how can we, as a transplanted people, bloom where we have been planted here in the United States? How can we ever re-attain the pre-eminence on the stage of world civilizations?

The same way you will succeed in school: with knowledge of self, self confidence, training and skills, and the willingness to work and get the job done.

The relatively few hardy Africans who survived the original African Holocaust caused by harsh environmental conditions, tribalism, famine and disease 5000 years ago were able to overcome these problems by thinking, planning, and working their way through the enormous difficulties they faced. Even when they weren't given the time to think, they had to take the time from somewhere.

Let's take a look at the lives of some of our ancestors.

Imhotep, an Egyptian, lived almost 3000 years before Jesus Christ was born. He is acknowledged as the real father of modern medicine who lived more than 2000 years before Hippocrates, a Greek doctor after whom today's Hippocratic oath is named. There is evidence that Imhotep and other Egyptian doctors diagnosed and treated more than 200 diseases. As such, Egypt was the acknowledged world leader in medicine as well as architecture. Later, the Greeks sent their doctors to Egypt to study medicine; compare that to today's situation where African students must go to Europe to study.

Akhenaton lived almost 3400 years ago. He preached a gospel of peace 1400 years before Christ, refusing to attack neighboring nations which would not pay tribute money to Egypt. He wrote poetry to God that rivals any of David's Psalms; a thousand years before Moses received the Ten Commandments from God, Akhenaton banned worship of graven images of bulls, cats and other animals in the land of Egypt. He believed firmly that there was only One True God, without form, who was the Unity which ran through all life. As best can be determined, he took only one wife with whom he had seven children. Most paintings show him with his family. His features, like that of his son Tutankahmen, (the boy king we know as "King Tut") are typically African: very thick lips, oblong head.

Hatsheptut, a Black woman pharaoh of Egypt who is called the greatest female ruler of all time. Aesop, a Black man who profoundly affected Western thought and morality. Hannibal, a Black man considered the greatest military mind ever, whose war tactics and strategies are still used on today's modern battlefields.

Phyliss Wheatley, a slave who later became a world-famous American poetess. Benjamin Banneker, a Black man who was a mathematical and mechanical genius chosen by U.S. President George Washington to design the Washington, D.C. street system.

James Derham, a slave who became America's first Black doctor and who was fluent in French, Spanish and English. Frederick Douglass, a former slave who physically whipped his former master and became one of the most eloquent Black spokesmen against slavery. Harriet Tubman, an illiterate ex-slave who was the greatest conductor on the slaves' Underground Railroad to freedom.

Booker T. Washington, who saw the future of Blacks becoming secured through vocational education and entry into the business and commercial world. W.E.B. DuBois, who believed in the development of a 'Talented Tenth' of Black intellectuals who would guide the Black community to the fulfillment of its highest potential.

Malcolm X, a high school dropout at 15, a convicted armed robber and dope dealer at 21, set the tone for a militant Black Power movement in the 1960's. Martin Luther King, Jr., a child of the Black middle class, used the power of his mind harnessed with supernatural faith to break the backbone of American segregation.

My brother or sister, these are your people. Six thousand years of history and leadership in a few pages. The best of us survived and proceeded to change the world.

Now tell me you can't make an A in calculus.

WHY YOU SHOULD HAVE CONFIDENCE IN YOURSELF

You are a success, even if you have never 'achieved' any of the goals you have set for yourself. You have been successful in your life and you may not even realize it.

How can this be?

First you are alive and well; at least you're well enough to be reading this book. That in and of itself is an accomplishment in today's world.

Secondly, you are motivated to improve yourself. I know that because you are reading these words, which means you are willing to invest your precious time to find out if you can learn how to be a better student.

Third and most importantly, you still have a relatively sound mind. That's the key to winning this game.

Everyone, and I do mean every human being on God's green earth, goes through changes and difficulties. If you look on any street

corner in America, you can see the result of the unwillingness to deal
with life's problems. That's right. Unwillingness, not inability.

Every conscious human act is an act of the WILL. You choose to
get angry at someone who curses you out in reaction to the other
person's action. Nobody makes you react.

You see people - street people, alcoholics, junkies, stockbrokers,
doctors, lawyers - who have chosen to solve their problems by opting
out of life. And don't let anybody fool you. Though some people are
truly physically or mentally unable to cope with life, many others have
chosen to give up the fight. Look at what is happening in the news on
a daily basis; high government officials, rich movie stars, and others
who seemingly have reached the pinnacle of American life are either
attempting or actually committing suicide. They deal with their problems by letting the problems overwhelm them, suck them in, to the
point of becoming an empty, burned-out husk of what they could
have been. Or they end up cold and dead, physically or emotionally.

The reason why this happens is simple: these people have lost
hope that things will get better. And when you lose hope, you may as
well be dead.

That has not happened to you, because you have not let the
everyday tedium of life get to you. Neither have you let the major
tragedies mow you down. To prove that to yourself, ask yourself this
question: "What is the hardest thing I have ever done, or the most difficult problem I have ever faced, in my life?"

The answer, of course, is different for different people. Whatever
the problem, the point is you've emerged from it, and you are still
around to tell the story.

Understand that success and survival are mostly learned behavior; academic success is no different. Many times, it is the painful
experiences that teach us how to survive bad times.

Mental survival through problem periods of your life provide what
I call individual points of reference. Simply put, that means that
you've succeeded at things that are tougher than the problem that

confronts you now. And since you've succeeded at the tougher thing, your current problem will be more easily hurdled.

Once you have established your point(s) of reference, you have overcome a major psychological hurdle. You have made a conscious decision to be a success and to change a defeatist attitude. That is the first step to be made in the continuing battle for academic success.

WINNING ATTITUDES AND ACTIONS

Dennis Waitley has identified ten qualities which exist in successful people, no matter what their races, religions, aims, goals, or professions. Five of these qualities are winning attitudes (**positive self-expectancy, positive self-image, positive self-control, positive self-esteem, and positive self-awareness**); five of Waitley's qualities are action qualities (**positive self-motivation, positive self-direction, positive self-discipline, positive self-dimension, and positive self-projection**). In an excellent audiotape entitled 'The Psychology of Winning' (Nightingale-Conant, Chicago, IL.) which is available at most bookstores, he describes them as follows:

POSITIVE SELF-EXPECTANCY: This can simply be described as optimism. Positive self-expectancy is expecting the most favorable result from your own action. Optimistic people with a positive self-expectancy look at problems as opportunities, and can always see the positive aspects of any difficulty. This attitude can be developed by making an effort to stay relaxed and friendly, no matter what the circumstances, and to be calm in all situations.

POSITIVE SELF-MOTIVATION : This is the action component, the inner drive that puts optimism into action.

According to Waitley, winners are driven by desire, rather than fear. Fear causes a person to dwell on the past, to think about the penalty of failure; fear restricts the person, and constantly causes the person to replay painful episodes in his mind.

Desire is the opposite of fear. Desire focuses the person's mind on the future, and directs the person's mind to dwell on the possible rewards for behavior. Desire attracts good things, and constantly replays successful episodes in the person's mind. A person with positive self-motivation concentrates on the desired results, not possible problems, and dwells on rewards, rather than penalties for failure.

To achieve positive self-motivation, try to replace fear with desire. For example, you can replace fear of poverty with the desire for financial wealth. You can replace fear of failure with desire for success.

POSITIVE SELF-IMAGE: The image that you have of yourself is a key attitude which will determine your success. People are controlled by their mental pictures at their subconscious level of awareness. According to Waitley, "It's not what you are that holds you back, it's what you think you're not." For example, all the plastic surgery in the world will not be helpful to a person whose mental concept of self is one of complete ugliness and self-loathing. You can begin to have a positive self-image by visualizing yourself as successful, i.e. by using the action quality, positive **self-direction**.

POSITIVE SELF-DIRECTION: This turns imagination into reality, and dreams into goals. If you have a positive self-image in which you visualize yourself being successful, you must set goals and accomplish them to make your vision come true.

Goal Setting and F.E.A.R.

Life forces us to make decisions everyday. Despite this, most people do not have clearly defined, written goals for their lives, usually as a consequence of fear. Zig Ziglar, a renowned salesman and motivational speaker, believes that FEAR stands for 'False Evidence Appearing Real'.

I believe that FEAR is the greatest obstacle facing Black students, and maybe even Black people world-wide. Fear causes most of Black folks' self-talk, the thoughts that run through our minds from second to second, to be negative. All our lives we are told that we cannot do certain things, and that the goals and desires we have set are unrealistic and a waste of time. Thus, many people fail to make goals because of fear of failure; other people fail to make goals because of fear of success, if they believe success will make friends and relatives jealous or uncomfortable.

Another major factor causing people not to set goals is poor self-image. In their wildest dreams, many people cannot imagine accomplishing anything. Positive thinking will not work for an individual who has a warped, totally negative image of himself.

Still other people have not set goals because they have never been convinced that setting a goal accomplishes any purpose.

For most students, lack of time for studying is not really the problem. The real problem is lack of direction.

In a series of audio tapes entitled 'Goals' (Nightingale Conant, Chicago, IL.), Ziglar describes a goal-setting process that will be helpful in determining positive self-direction. Setting goals gives direction, which frees time. Ziglar suggests the following procedure:

1. Develop a wild idea list. List everything you ever want to be, do, or have.

2. Let the wild idea list sit for 24 or 48 hours, and add any other wild ideas that come to mind. By this time, you should have everything you ever wanted to do on this list.

3. Shorten the list, but do not throw it away. Your aim in shortening the list is to "say no to some good goals, so that you can yes to the best goals," according to Ziglar. Certain goals, though they may be good, are not priorities, and can be worked on later.

4. Categorize the remaining goals into the following categories: physical, mental, spiritual, social, financial, and family. A well-rounded person has goals that encompass each of these categories.

5. For each remaining goal listed, ask yourself the following questions: Will reaching this goal make me happier? If the goal is one that will provide pleasure, can I repeat this pleasure indefinitely and be happy as a result? Will accomplishment of this goal make me healthier? More prosperous? Will accomplishment of this goal give

me peace of mind? Improve my family relationships?

If this goal is to remain as a goal, you must answer <u>yes</u> to at least <u>one</u> of each of the preceding questions for every goal.

6. <u>Further categorize the goals into long-range, short-range, and daily goals.</u>

7. <u>Set ongoing goals, such as maintaining a positive self-image, staying healthy, and maintaining a loving relationship with your spouse, family, or other loved ones.</u> Make them specific! According to Waitley, "What you set is what you get." The mind does not respond to general statements, such as "I'd like to lose weight." Set specific goals: "I'd like to lose 25 pounds; I want to make an 'A' in Mathematics; I want to make a 'B' in English Composition."

8. <u>Check all your goals, and ask yourself these questions:</u> Are the goals just out of reach (which is OK), or are they out of sight? All of your goals must be realistic. Realistic goals do not depend on luck for their accomplishment. Ziglar says that unrealistic goals are the seed bed of depression and frustration.

9. <u>Ask yourself the following questions:</u> Are these my goals? Note that it is almost impossible to achieve goals that other people have set for you. You must set and accomplish your own goals, not those of your parents, teachers, or others.

Is this goal morally right and fair to everyone concerned? Will accomplishment of this goal take you closer to or further from your major objective? Can you emotionally commit yourself to start and finish this project, and do everything needed to accomplish this goal? Can you literally see yourself accomplishing this goal?

10. <u>Attempt to work all of your goals down to about four or five goals, in addition to your regular daily goals.</u> This will usually be a reasonable number for you to accomplish at any one time.

11. <u>Take inventory of where you are right now.</u> (See the self-assessment process described a little later in this chapter.)

12. <u>List all the benefits that accomplishment of every listed goal will bring you.</u>

13. Once your goals are set, ask yourself some more questions: Have your goals been written down? Have you spelled out why you want to accomplish these goals? Have you identified the obstacles that you must overcome to achieve your goals? Have you identified what you need to know in order to achieve your goals? Have you identified the people, organizations, or groups that you need to work with in order to accomplish your goals? Have you designed a concrete plan of action to accomplish your goals?

Ziglar estimates that it should take you anywhere between 10 and 20 hours to set your goals and devise a plan to accomplish them. If the goals and plans are complex, it might take longer.

Following Through on Goals

Once goals and plans are set, the work really begins.

1. Make a real commitment to achieve your goals. There are going to be times when you do everything right and you still do not accomplish your goal. Where do you go from there? When obstacles arise, learn how to change the direction of how to accomplish your goals, but do not change your decision to accomplish your goals. People who consistently accomplish goals learn how to respond positively to disappointments and obstacles.

2. Keep a daily detailed account of the progress that you have made toward accomplishment of the goals. However, don't confuse activity with accomplishment. Just because you are busy doesn't mean you are doing work which will lead to accomplishing your goal. A caged hamster on a treadmill generates a lot of activity, but goes nowhere.

3. At the end of every day, make a list of things that you have done with your time. At the same time, you can make your plans for what you will do tomorrow. A convenient time to do this is ten minutes just before bed. If you fail to do this, you quickly lose sight of the goals, and the probability of failure increases.

Before you leave home for the day, consider placing your activity planner, or whatever you are using to keep track of your goals, under the pillow. When you get ready to go to bed, you will see your planner on the pillow and will remember to review the activities of the day, and to make plans for tomorrow.

4. <u>List the most important things you have to do tomorrow morning, from the most difficult to the easiest.</u> When you get up in the morning, work on the number one task on the list <u>first</u>.

5. <u>Keep these other things in mind:</u>

A. If you're going to start toward accomplishment of the goal, you must start with a solid foundation. That foundation includes trust, honesty, integrity, perseverance. If this means getting right with God, then do so.

B. Start the goal-setting process today. It is the series of little things that you do on a daily basis that determine whether you accomplish the goal. Divide the activities necessary to accomplish your goal into small bites.

C. Do <u>not</u> become a person who is susceptible to the negative influences of other people. Though you may not have accomplished all of your goals, you must not begin to lower your goals because other goals have not been accomplished.

D. Do <u>not</u> allow other people to set your goals for you, or place mental burdens upon you, which will prevent you from giving 100% effort toward accomplishment of your goals.

E. Know your time. Be a time miser, particularly with regard to television. Get a Sunday paper, circle those programs you which to watch, watch them, and turn the TV off immediately after the program is over. Alternatively, you could record the program you wish to watch, and schedule a time later on when you can see that program, and that program <u>only</u>, at your convenience.

F. Focus on the accomplishments you can make. You must literally see yourself achieving the goals you have set.

G. Once a week, look at and review all of your goals on your goals list. Decide which goals you should work on during the week. At the end of each day, you should have done some activity toward accomplishment of that goal that you have picked for the week. If you allow two days to pass by consecutively in which you have not worked on a weekly goal, you're in trouble.

H. Decide whether to share your goals with someone else. According to Ziglar, share your 'go-up' goals only with those people whom you believe will encourage and help you to achieve your goals. For example, a goal to be the #1 student in the class should be shared with the teacher, rather than another student, because another student may be considered a competitor. Share 'give up' goals, i.e. giving up smoking or drinking, etc., with everyone you know, so that they will help you put pressure on yourself.

I. There is a definite positive correlation between success and physical exercise. People who consistently exercise also seem to be able to set and accomplish their goals more easily.

J. Whenever you accomplish one goal, immediately set a new one from your list.

POSITIVE SELF-CONTROL: This is an attitude that winners have, that make them believe that they are in control of their lives. According to Waitley, "Winners make it happen, while losers let it happen."

All conscious human activity is volitional, which means that you decide to do things on your own. No one makes you get up in the morning, go to school, go to work, or anything else. You even have control over whether you live or die. Nobody makes you rob somebody, steal something, or put drugs in your veins. Each person must reach a form of maturity, and become responsible for his or her own actions.

POSITIVE SELF-DISCIPLINE: This quality puts positive self-control into action. Consider reprogramming your conscious mind with thoughts of self-control, success, and positive self-images. This is done by self-discipline, which involves practice, practice, practice. Just as a tree grows from the inside, layer by layer, our thoughts also grow one layer at a time. You must begin to put new thoughts into your minds, one thought at a time, and reinforce these thoughts, minute by minute, on a daily basis. Positive self-discipline involves committing yourself to thinking new thoughts and habits, and relentlessly repeating them everyday.

Everyday, visualize accomplishment of the goal, whatever it is. If your goal is losing ten pounds, you must visualize yourself ten pounds lighter, and squeezing into that brand new bathing suit. If your goal is improving your basketball free throw percentage, you must visualize yourself shooting the perfect free throw in your mind, time after time. If it's making an 'A' on a Math test, you must visualize yourself sitting for the exam, knowing every formula, and correctly answering each question, so that you can make an 'A'.

Your new positive thought patterns must become the dominant thoughts in your mind. Even when you do not reach your goals, and fall short of all desired performance, criticize yourself in a positive manner. Rather than saying "I'm dumb, stupid, and should have done better", tell yourself that you did well, that you will learn from the mistakes that you made, and that next time you will do better. Then, continue the visualization of the positive results, and rehearse everything as if you have already mastered it.

POSITIVE SELF-ESTEEM: Winners who have decided to like themselves, and feel that they are worthwhile persons. A person with positive self-esteem would rather be themselves than anybody else in the world.

Positive self-esteem is learned through practice. Actions you can take which will build your positive self-esteem include using affirmations and constructive self-talk, i.e. building yourself up even when you make mistakes (I am a strong person, I can be successful, I will lose ten pounds, etc.); accepting all compliments with a thank-you, rather than telling the person who complimented you that you don't deserve it; and dressing the best that you can at all times, since looking good physically makes you feel better emotionally.

When meeting people, tell them your name first, proudly and boldly. Walk tall and briskly ; if you are in a class or in a seminar, try to sit up front, if at all possible. Enjoy yourself, indulge yourself on occasion, and don't be ashamed to do so.

POSITIVE SELF-DIMENSION: When you put positive self-esteem into action, project it into everyday living, your self-dimension then becomes positive. Waitley describes having a positive self-dimension as "being in harmony with the divine order of things, and having a keen awareness of the value of time." Old folks call it 'getting right with God.' A person with a positive selfdimension realizes that growing old is a state of mind, and enjoys life, while taking care of his body, and setting goals which benefits others, as well as himself.

POSITIVE SELF-AWARENESS: A person with this attitude accepts his uniqueness as a person, and knows his strengths and weaknesses. He is able to place himself in others' situations in an attempt to understand as they do.

POSITIVE SELF-PROJECTION: A winner holds herself out as a winner, and projects a winner's aura. The image that people see of us tells them a lot of what goes on in our minds. People who are satisfied with their looks, their state of mind, and their path in life, are generally happier and are more confident people. Winners project constructive support of ideas, and can differ with people without destructive criticism. A person with positive self-projection can help other people solve their problems. In solving their problems, the winner can reach goals of her own.

DEVELOPING SUPPORT SYSTEMS

Support systems can be defined as almost anything or anybody that can keep you going when you want to throw in the towel. For the purposes of this book, we shall refer only to an academic/psychological support system, not a financial support system.

Let me say that drugs or drinking should not be considered part of anyone's academic support system, for a number of reasons, most of which you already know.

A WORD ABOUT PLEASURE

Physical pleasure is addictive. Physical pleasure can be simply defined as anything that feels good to your body; eating food, lounging in hot tubs, drinking alcohol, to name a few things. There is nothing wrong with anything on the preceding list in and of itself, if done in moderation.

But before you get upset and accuse me of being an alcohol soaked, sex-crazed junkie, let me say something. In all behavior, we must consider the consequences of and circumstances surrounding our actions.

Example: Is sex wrong? Is partying wrong? No, in and of themselves. Then why shouldn't you have sex with whomever, whenever, and wherever you want? Because of the possible consequences, or effects, of that willful decision. What are possible consequences of sex without planning, or spiritual, legal, and emotional commitment? Unwanted pregnancy, sexually transmitted diseases, emotional pain. What are the possible consequences of non-stop partying? Academic failure, the embarrassment of parents and friends, financial hardship and obligations to repay school loans for nothing: more emotional pain.

The bottom line: always consider the consequences and circumstances of your actions! The consequences of doing drugs are addiction and possible death. The consequence of legal drinking under improper circumstances (i.e. while driving) is jail; the consequence of cooling out in a hot tub under improper circumstances (i.e.while your teacher is passing out a test) is failure.

Of course, it is your right to disagree with my analysis. But believe me you are dumb, dumb, dumb to add anything to your support system that has a high possibility of becoming compulsive or addictive.

I have seen brothers and sisters who have literally screwed or partied their way onto academic probation and eventually out of school. Why? Because they couldn't keep their dresses down or their zippers up, or because they could not pass by a party. These types of behaviors are just as compulsive and addictive as any illegal drug, and can have the same devastating effect on self-esteem and self-confidence.

INTERNAL SUPPORT SYSTEM

Your internal support system is the thoughts, emotions, and

intellectual and spiritual processes that will help you through hard times. This is probably the more important of the support components. So many times, you will get discouraged and disappointed. Maybe you can't get in contact with a friend or parent; maybe you were able to talk to them, but it didn't help. It is then that you may be forced to look within yourself and tap into the God-given reservoir of strength that we all have. As a result, many students find that prayer or meditation is an indispensable factor in their support system.

EXTERNAL SUPPORT SYSTEM

External parts of your support system include family and friends, your church, classmates, spouses, etc. I call it 'external' because it's outside your body, as contrasted with internal, which is inside the mind.

Many times, your external support system is very informal and intuitive. Most people have at least one good friend with whom they can discuss anything. This person is probably part of your support system, an outlet for blowing off steam, a willing ear to share triumphs and tragedies. At major colleges, the school psychologist serves this purpose. It is important to be able to get a pat on the back or a sympathetic ear.

Fraternities and campus organizations can be very important components of your external support system. They provide that camaraderie that comes with common interests.

However, be careful that you are not sucked in by negative peer pressure. Your first obligation is not to the club, organization or fraternity. Somebody is paying good money for your education; that somebody may be you. You are not in school to be cool or necessarily to be accepted by your classmates. You are there to learn and to prepare yourself for life after school.

LEARNING TO TURN MINUSES INTO PLUSES

I firmly believe that fear of failure and embarrassment is one of the major emotions that plague Black students every day of their academic existence; in class, on exams, and in study groups. The reasons why are easy to understand: pride, high expectations of family and friends, and low expectations of instructors and classmates.

However, fear of failure, anger, and other 'negative' emotions can also be part of your internal support system, if you tie them in with your more positive attitudes and emotions, such as pride and self-confidence. How? By forcing you to lift yourself from the morass of self-pity, doubt, laziness, procrastination, or depression in which you may find yourself.

Let me give you a personal example.

There were times in the University of Florida's Master of Business Administration (MBA) program that I literally cried; failed Accounting tests, class participation embarrassments, and on and on. But what kept me going was fear of failure. I refused, because of pride and ego, to let anyone say that I flunked out of school. When I would visualize myself telling close friends that I couldn't cut the mustard; when I saw in my mind's eye the smirks on the faces of instructors and classmates who told me I couldn't do it; I would quit feeling sorry for myself and redouble my efforts.

Be aware, however, that you have to have confidence in yourself and the willingness to work to the limits of your physical, mental and emotional endurance for this approach to work. Otherwise this 'visualization of failure' approach will kill you by sinking you deeper and deeper into depression and self-pity.

Now I know that this approach is directly contrary to the 'visualization of success' that was described earlier. But remember one of the premises on which this book is written: DO WHAT WORKS FOR YOU. This tactic worked for me, and still does.

PRACTICING STRESS REDUCTION TECHNIQUES

Notice that the subject here is stress reduction rather than stress elimination.

First, it is impossible to eliminate external stress from your environment, since you have a limited amount of control over this environment. You can't control crime, traffic, or other people. Thus, you do the best you can to cope with the stress that you cannot control, while making every effort you can to reduce or eliminate those stressful situations that are within your control.

The major stress factor within your control is physical stress. Literally, too much anxiety will kill you physically and academically. A regular program of physical exercise is highly recommended, especially exercise with some aerobic benefit, such as riding a bicycle to class every day.

Eating the proper food is also important. While in grad school, I became a part-time vegetarian, which helped keep my weight down.

For relaxation, I highly recommend yoga-type exercise that emphasize flexibility within your body's limits, and because it is a discipline that makes you very aware of your body, much like biofeedback. If you know what your body feels like when it is relaxed, you know what it feels like when it is tense. During an exam, you can take a quick 'inventory' of your body for tenseness and, if necessary, relax that portion of your anatomy by force of will. A very powerful technique!

By now, you have probably developed your own method of dealing with stress. If you have, continue to use the methods that work for you. Again, let me emphasize that drugs have no place in my suggested program. I'll suggest only grudgingly that you go out for a beer with some friends, maybe as a reward for your hard work; I only suggest this because alcohol is legal in this society, if not consumed to excess. You are aware, I am sure, that alcohol is a drug. The main danger is the possibility of both physical and psychological addiction that was mentioned earlier.

Ah, but what of emotional and mental stress? Again, the key is to eliminate the causes of stress that you can, and manage the causes of stress that cannot be eliminated.

Note that it is the causes of stress that should be examined; for example, if you absolutely bug out at the thought of being called on in class, you should immediately ask yourself why.

Different causes call for different solutions. If you are afraid because you are unprepared, the obvious solution is to prepare to respond before you get to class. However, if you get extremely nervous because you may be self-conscious about a dialect or the sound of your own voice before an audience, the solution is different. Maybe a public speaking course will help; maybe asking and answering questions aloud in front of a mirror may help. Other suggestions include practicing in front of trusted friends whose criticism and judgment you trust, or recording your voice so that you can evaluate the sound of it yourself. Maybe just coming to terms with how you speak is the answer.

Here are some other things you can do to reduce stress:

Adopt and maintain an objective attitude. Try not to take every bad thing that happens to you so personally. Don't get mad about everything that happens, particularly things you can't change.

Evaluate your own behavior objectively. Are you causing your own pain and disappointment? What can you do or change about yourself that can make your life better?

Assume an active attitude. Inaction, laziness, and pessimism breeds hopelessness, which leads to frustration, anger, and resentment. Concentrate on making the difference by your personal participation. Light a candle, rather than curse the darkness.

Live in the present. Be aware of the past. Learn from the past. Live for today and use your time wisely. Make plans for tomorrow.

Develop a sense of humor. Even in the midst of daily pain and chaos, life is funny. There is plenty to laugh about every day, especially in school.

Don't work all the time. Reward yourself for personal achievement. Try to set aside some time every day to do something you like, just for yourself.

Substitute planning for worry. Plan your work, then work your plan. If you have a good plan for accomplishment of your goals, you can

If you have a good plan for accomplishment of your goals, you can direct your energy toward achievement, rather than squandering time worrying about failure. PRIOR PLANNING PREVENTS POOR PERFORMANCE.

Specific answers to specific problems of emotional stress such as marital problems, etc. are beyond the scope of this book. But much of the stress you will face in your academic environment is related to your level of preparation. You'd be surprised at how your level of anxiety decreases as your level of academic preparation increases.

But no matter what happens, always, always do your best. Be satisfied in your mind, heart and soul that you could have done no more to prepare for the task ahead.

Also, the 'visualization of failure' technique should be used in conjunction with 'visualization of success' that was describe earlier, for the greatest positive benefits. That way, as your mind helps you to avoid the pain of failure, you also are working toward achieving your visualization of success.

This tactic worked for me, and still does. Little did I know that a man named Anthony Robbins had developed a program for success called <u>Neuro-associative Conditioning Systems</u>™ that uses both visualization techniques in a conscious manner, just as I had been instinctively using them during my school days.

In a series of audiotapes called <u>Personal Power</u> (Guthy-Renker Corp., Irwindale, CA), Robbins thoroughly explains his belief that it is links in our minds that are made between pain and pleasure that determine behavior. He believes that to change behavior, we must change the links between a given behavior and the reward or pain we enjoy or suffer as a consequence of the behavior.

Suppose, for example, that a student has a belief that he cannot pass a math class because he has never been good with numbers. For someone interested in a career in engineering or science, this could be a belief that devastates his life, and prevents him from doing something he always wanted to do. This belief about not being good with numbers may have been a reaction to flunking a few

math tests in elementary school, or not being able to easily understand math concepts. Whatever the particular facts, this student's
low opinion about his abilities is probably a consequence of FEAR
(False Evidence Appearing Real), that we identified earlier.

How can this limiting belief be changed? Robbins suggests using
the Dickens Pattern. This technique is named after Charles Dickens,
author of the classic book entitled A Christmas Carol. In that book,
Ebenezer Scrooge is a stingy, selfish man who hates Christmas. In
order to change his present behavior, three ghosts (the ghosts of
Christmas past, present and future) travel with him through time and
survey his life in an effort to convince Scrooge to change his present
behavior.

Here is Robbins' Dickens' Pattern:

1. Identify your limiting beliefs.
2. Ask: What has this belief cost me in the past? How does that make
   me feel?
3. Ask: What is this belief costing me today? How does that make me
   feel?
4. Imagine yourself 5 years from today.
5. Ask: What will this belief have cost me emotionally, physically,
   financially, in my relationships?
6. Dragging the pain of this belief with you forward, step into the
   future, 10 years from today.
7. Ask: What will this belief have cost me emotionally, physically,
   financially, in my relationships?
8. Recognize and rejoice that none of this has happened yet, and
   literally shake it off. Change your body radically: Move as if you
   felt totally energized, excited, and vital. Breathe more rapidly.
9. Determine what new, empowering belief you must adopt.
10. Step into the future 10 years from today.
11. Ask: What have I gained from this belief (10 years in the future)?
    How does that make me feel?
12. Ask: How this belief made my life greater and more enjoyable?
    How does that make me feel?
13. Look at both destinies and decide which one you are committed

to creating, and mentally return to the present, compelled to act on your new choice.

Robbins' series of audiotapes, which he markets as a '30-day program for unlimited success', is one of the best systems I have seen anywhere to develop the skills necessary for personal achievement. At a price of almost $200 (as of this writing), it is on the expensive side for someone on a student budget. However, I highly recommend it anyway, as I do the audiotapes by Waitley and Ziglar. The relatively small investment in time and money you will expend to buy and learn these systems will pay off in higher self-esteem and self-confidence and better grades.

MAKING A SELF-ASSESSMENT: TAKING A GOOD LOOK AT YOU

Self-assessment is a critical but difficult part of our preseason conditioning program. Self-assessment can be described as mentally stepping outside of your body, appraising yourself, and determining your strengths and weaknesses as objectively as possible. (I said it wasn't easy.)

The reason self-assessment is critical is that only when you sit in judgment and evaluate yourself can you determine if you have the necessary endurance, desire and discipline to run and finish the academic marathon. And make no mistake: academia is a marathon, not a sprint! If you are not willing to sign up for the duration, don't even bother.

Self-assessment is no mystical process, however. We do it all the time when we constructively criticize ourselves and make a promise to do better. Can you count the number of New Year's resolutions you have made? They were probably due to some shortcoming you perceived about yourself or some goal you knew you had the possibility of obtaining.

Suppose one student's academic self-assessment reveals this student: (1) has a knee-shaking fear of numbers, because of carelessness and inattention (2) writes well and is comfortable taking essay exams (3) enjoys arguing with people and is verbally quick (4) works fairly well under tight time constraints (5) a glutton for punishment and will study all day and night to prepare for an exam (6) has no discipline (7) is a party animal (8) studies better with a partner than alone (9) is a very proud person who finds it difficult to ask a question.

Obviously, such a person would find it difficult to major in mathematics, for a number of reasons. Let me say here, however, that nowhere in this book will you read the word impossible, because I believe that it is possible to achieve any academic goal.

Assuming that this person decided to major in math anyway, is he or she willing to pay the price to achieve academic success, given the difficulties to be faced? Is this person willing to develop disciplined study habits instead of cramming? Work problem after problem? To squarely confront his or her fear of numbers, determine the cause, and work to eliminate it? Do those weaknesses in the skills most important to success in math outweigh personal strengths? Is the motive for choosing this major (i.e., money, ego, etc.) powerful enough to make all the studying worthwhile?

These are only a few of the questions every serious student should ask during self-assessment:

What strengths and weaknesses do I have academically? Do I have strong writing, verbal, or numerical skills? Do I have a good basic foundation for using the English language? Do I have solid, disciplined study habits?

What are my personality traits? Am I a loner or a 'people person'? Aggressive or shy? Hard-working or lazy? Impulsive or deliberate?

Am I highly motivated to achieve the academic goals I have set for myself? If not, why not? If so, is the motivation internal (ego, pride, sense of accomplishment) or external (community or professional status, money, etc.)?

Am I willing to throw out bad habits that I am comfortable with, if necessary, to achieve my academic goals? If not, why not?

Where does finishing school fit on my list of life's priorities? Is getting a degree really important to me?

Am I willing to 'sweat' to achieve my academic goals? Will I study long hours; cut back on recreational activities; make financial and personal sacrifices, if necessary, to be a successful student?

Am I willing to sacrifice ego and control over my academic life in order to achieve success? It is this question that poses so many of us independent thinkers real problems in school.

PRINCIPLE vs EGO: WHEN TO TURN THE OTHER CHEEK

Many times, Black students have to decide to either stand up for what we may perceive as racist behavior, or to ignore, forget, and move on. This a tough decision to make.

Rather than give you an ironclad rule to follow in these situations, I'll just tell you the differences between principle and egotism.

Let's define principle as a fundamental rule or code of conduct by which you live your life. A primary principle for most people is respect for self and others.

Egotism is defined as an exaggerated sense of the person's importance. An egotistic person is convinced that the world revolves around him and him alone, and his (or her) moral standards are higher than the standards of the rest of the world. Egotism is self-respect that becomes conceit and arrogance.

Egotism and principle overlap, and it is basically a matter of degree. You will be faced with situations that will be racially motivated if you are in a white school, and they will be subtle. Such situations may include never getting called on in class; being frozen out of study group discussion; never receiving an invitation to a classmate's weekend party. Remember, you can choose your reaction to these situations! NEVER let anybody manipulate you into jumping to their tune. If you decide to raise hell, ask yourself whether a die-hard, live-or-die principle is involved, or merely ego. Ask yourself whether getting upset and launching a verbal attack against an instructor or student will serve a valid purpose. (Sometimes it does.) Then, you decide for yourself how to react, given the circumstances.

You now know how to assess yourself. Once you have completed your self-assessment, find out from an informed source what it takes to succeed in your desired major or career path. If your self-assessment matches the requirements for the particular major or career you have chosen, you have a much higher probability of success. If the match is a poor one, you should consider your motivational level in tackling the major or career, because a lot more effort will be required of you.

Using the previous example of the math major described above, it seems that this person may be more suited to another major that may not be so numbers-oriented, such as journalism. However, if this individual decides to stick with math, it must be recognized that the road to success will be long, hard, rocky, and probably difficult, but never, <u>ever</u> impossible.

Only you can decide if the race is worth running and winning, given the demands school will make on you. If you decide to run the academic race, then run to win!

SUMMARY

You are a part of a people with a history of more than just survival. Black people have excelled, because of persistence and imagination, throughout world history under worse conditions you will face in any academic program, no matter how difficult.

In your life you have faced difficulties before, and you have successfully overcome them.

Successful people all over the world have winning ATTITUDES (positive self-expectancy, self-image, self-control, self-esteem, self-awareness) that eventually become ACTIONS (positive self-motivation, self-direction, self-discipline, self-dimension, self-projection).

Goal-setting is critical. You MUST spend time developing a set of realistic goals, and regularly evaluate whether you are accomplishing these goals.

Make an investment in yourself by buying information that will help you become successful (Waitley, Ziglar, Robbins).

Develop internal (God/spiritual) support and external (friends, other people) support systems.

Beware of any physical pleasure than can become addictive and lead to misplaced priorities: sex, drugs, etc.

Turn fear of academic failure and its consequences into a positive motivator to go the extra mile.

Physical exercise and diet and preparation for school can help reduce stress.

Objectively assess yourself to determine your academic strengths and weaknesses.

Check your ego at the classroom door.

CHAPTER FOUR

GATHERING THE EQUIPMENT

Education must enable one to sift and weigh evidence, to discern the true from the false, the real from the unreal, and the facts from fiction. The function of education, therefore, is to teach one to think intensively and to think critically. But education which stops with efficiency may prove the greatest menace to society. The most dangerous criminal may be the man gifted with reason but with no morals.

Martin Luther King, Jr.

Your preseason conditioning is now complete. It is time to learn the specific skills every student should have. Many times these skills make the difference in the quality of the educational experience; that is, whether it is drudgery or delight.

My goal in writing this book is to let you in on the 'secrets' of successful studying. This means learning how to study with effectiveness and efficiency. Effectiveness is accomplishing the goals you have set; efficiency is accomplishing the goals using the least amount of time and energy. Students who enjoy their school years are usually efficient, which allows them to enjoy lots of the extracurricular activities that make the whole experience fun. Students who are effective get the academic honors, the respect of their instructors and peers, and eventually more money in their respective careers.

This chapter will briefly outline tools primarily used to increase your efficiency and will be useful to you throughout life. If you want more information on specific techniques, refer to the particular book which is cited in either the text or the List of References.

A SPECIAL NOTE ON WHY GRADES ARE IMPORTANT

According to a 1977 study of Black students by Dr. Charles V. Willie and Arline Sakuma McCord, Black Students at White Colleges (New York: Praeger Publishers, 1977), the Black college freshman had the hardest time of all racial groups and class levels in achieving scholastic goals. Only 14% of Black freshman achieved a 'B' average after first semester, compared to 47% of the white freshman. During the second and third years of school, Black students improved at a higher rate than did whites, finally catching up during senior year.

One can conclude from this study that the Black students got off on the wrong foot, and had to work like hell for the next three years to catch up. One major reason they had to work so hard is because mathematically, your grade point average (GPA) is weighted toward your freshman year.

Because you start off with a clean slate (no grades) during your freshman year, you set the numerical standard for your academic career. If you start off flunking classes, you have to work twice as hard to improve as you take more and more classes. If you start off making A's every course, you have to really work hard to flunk out as you take more and more classes.

Let's say you are at the end of your freshman year at a four-year college on the 4-point grading scale (A=4 points, B=3 points, C=2 points, D=1 point, F=zero). You have taken 30 hours of classes and have flunked every one of them. Therefore your GPA is zero; total points (30 hours x zero points) divided by the number of hours (30). You have an F average.

If you were going to pull your GPA up to a 'B' average, you would have to take 120 hours worth of classes, or 40-three hour courses, and make A's in every one of them to pull your GPA up. That means that you would not even get close to the 'B' range till your senior year!

The reason why is because <u>the more classes you take, the harder it is for your GPA to be affected, either up or down, by grades in the future.</u> Let's look at another example.

Suppose you were in the same school, and at the end of your freshman year you took the same 30 hours of classes and made all A's. Your GPA would be total points (30 hours x 4 points) divided by the number of hours (30), or 120 divided by 30, which equals 4. You have an 'A' average.

Because your GPA is so high, you could make all C's your sophomore year, assuming you take 30 hours, and still keep a 'B' average. If you play around with the numbers a little, you'll get the idea of what I'm talking about.

To make a long story short, DON'T GET BEHIND IN YOUR GRADES EARLY. It will cause you much grief if you aren't serious right from the beginning. If you don't have the 'A' or 'B' average by the end of sophomore year, you are gonna have to work long days and nights to get those kinds of grades. If you are in high school, it works the same way.

Another important factor is the lag time between making grades and averaging them into your overall GPA on your transcript. This is a problem when you are applying for college, graduate or professional schools, because you usually apply during October or November of your senior year.

If you have waited until senior year to bear down on grades, the school you have applied for won't see those straight A's you waited so long to make because they won't be posted on your transcript until January. Colleges, universities, graduate and professional schools, depending on the number of applications, have already made many of their selections by then. Your second semester A's won't be posted until just before or just after you graduate, so the school for which you have applied will never see them.

Lag time could also affect your eligibility for academic scholarships and awards. So don't hang out during freshman year and try to catch up later.

THE CRITICAL TOOLS

ACTIVE, AGGRESSIVE LISTENING

Listening is one of the most underrated factors of student success, because it is such a crucial part of the information gathering process. Without good listening skills, it is almost impossible to do well in school.

Before going any further, let me define listening and hearing.

Webster's New Collegiate Dictionary defines listening as "hearing with thoughtful attention." Hearing is defined as "the process, function, or power of perceiving sound." By these definitions, we can see that the difference is when you are listening, you are paying attention.

Experts in human communication have come up with some statistics that will surprise you.

On the average,people spend about 70 percent of their time communicating in one form or another. Of this 70 percent, it is estimated that about nine percent is devoted to writing, 16 percent to reading, 30 percent to talking, and about 45 percent to listening. And when we listen, we really retain only about 25 percent of what we have listened to.

Why is that true? Because we HAVEN'T listened. We have only HEARD. If you add up those numbers, it means that we only truly listen to an average of 10 percent of what is said to us over a lifetime.

The key to listening is aggression and involvement. As we know, it is so much easier to accomplish something that you are totally involved in, mind, body and soul. Listening is the same way.

Try this: next time you have a conversation with somebody, lean forward and look at them intently. Hang on to every word the person says. If you do this, you probably won't have a problem understanding what the person is saying. You'll also probably be able to recall what was said quicker and more easily.

This should be the posture of a student who is listening, not just hearing, a teacher's lecture. The student's attention should be focused totally on what the teacher is saying.

And just like every other skill, listening CAN be learned. We will concentrate on developing listening skills specifically for purposes of class lectures. Here is what you can do:

1. Prepare to listen. Do your homework on the instructor or speaker, as well as the topic of the speech, if you know what it is.
To prepare your mind to receive the information to be presented to you, you need a road map, or at least some expectation of what to expect. This can come from the class syllabus or outline, as well as from the Table of Contents of the book from which the instructor is lecturing.

If a guest speaker is scheduled to appear, you can ask your instructor in advance for information about the speaker. Then, go to the library and find some biographical information about the speaker, if it is available.

For further information, review the section below on "Keeping Track of Class Lectures."

2. Be a receptive listener. Restrain your emotions, if necessary.
You may hate the class or the topic. You may even hate the instructor or the speaker. So what? Your purpose for listening is to receive information that will allow you to learn and to perform on the exam.

If you find yourself with an attitude that will prevent you from concentrating on getting information from the speaker, ask yourself why you are paying somebody's hard-earned money to go to school. Are you there to be entertained by the speaker? If so, you ought to quit school and spend your money on movie tickets.

Be mature enough to understand that learning ain't always pleasant. Sometimes it's hard work and occasionally it's painful. But YOU must decide that you will not let your feelings dictate whether the learning process will be successful.

3. Adjust to the speaker. How is the speaker's delivery? Is it as slow as molasses or rapid-fire? Each presents different problems. If it is slow,

your mind has a tendency to wander as you wait for the speaker to 'catch up'. If his delivery is rapid-fire, you have to consistently pay attention and take good notes or you may miss something. Either way, it is up to you to adjust, since the speaker is giving information you want. Some speakers and instructors could care less if they bore you to tears or if they leave you more confused. If that happens, speak up and ask questions. Make sure you do understand what they are trying to say.

4. Concentrate. Sometimes easier said than done. Force yourself to listen actively, even if the speaker's fly is open or her slip is showing. The only way to concentrate is to concentrate. If you find yourself daydreaming, mentally pull yourself out of it.

5. Summarize and filter the speech or lecture. Learn to recognize signal words and phrases. Keep what you believe is important, what the speaker emphasizes is important, and throw the rest away.

Usually, a speech or lecture is made up of a few main points and numerous subtopics. These are woven into the speech's introduction, the theme or premise, the body, and the conclusion. Sometimes you can get a clear road map right away from the title of the speech, if the speaker gives you one. Example: "I have entitled my speech MANHOOD, SCHOLARSHIP, PERSEVERANCE, AND UPLIFT: FOUR PRINCIPLES FOR SUCCESSFUL LIVING." The premise is clear; the speaker believes that those four qualities lead to successful living. He will probably provide information on subtopics on each of those four principles in the body of the speech.

Listen for clues, like necessary, crucial, important. Words like these indicate that the speaker thinks this information is important. Words like in addition to, first, second, next in order indicate a major idea. Finally, in conclusion and in summary indicate a summarization of all important ideas may be forthcoming.

KEEPING TRACK OF CLASS LECTURES

Reading textbooks are only a part of the learning and exam preparation process. Almost every instructor will supplement, modify or rebut principles found in the book during class lectures. Thus, it is important to have a record of what was said in class so that your understanding is increased. Having a record of the lecture also gives you an idea of what the instructor thinks are the more important portions of the subject.

There are two basic forms of preserving the class lecture: (a) electronic, either video or audio; (b) manual class notes.

These days, electronic recording of lectures is not unusual. Many large colleges and universities have so many students enrolled in the lower level introductory 'weed-out' courses (such as Intro to Business, Math, Biology, etc.), that lectures must be videotaped. This tape is then shown to classes that meet later in the day so that more students can complete the course. Such a system is great, of course, for the school, which can teach more students with fewer teachers. It is lousy for students because there's no instructor to immediately answer questions.

However, if your class is videotaped, you can use that to your advantage. The videotape can act as your backup system to your class notes, which you should be taking anyway. I would suggest that you not get into the habit of always checking your notes against the taped lecture. You are wasting time that could be more profitably spent reading, sleeping, partying (as a reward for diligent study), or determining how to save the world.

Checking your notes against the tape means that you will have to sit through the lecture all over again if the portion you missed was near the end of the lecture. Usually the tapes are shown at set times only to groups of students during the day, so you cannot get the tape and fast-forward or rewind it to the proper position. Therefore, it's best to get it right the first time, if you can.

For the same reason, I would not suggest audiotaping a class. It is a true time-waster most of the time. The audiotapes become a hassle to keep up with because they will multiply on you like rabbits if you try to tape all your classes. Get it right in class the first time. If you miss something, ask the instructor, then ask classmates.

TAKING WRITTEN NOTES

Unfortunately some students, like myself, couldn't take good notes to save our lives. Others had absolutely marvelous note-taking skills. It is important to understand that notetaking is a means to an end, rather than a goal in itself. Notes don't have to be cute or neat or good-looking or works of art. Taking class notes is simply a way to get an accurate account of the instructor's lecture, nothing more.

Therefore, if you have a note-taking system that is well-organized and it works for you, stick with it. If you have problems with notes, or if you want some ideas on how to improve your existing note-taking system, here is a brief survey of various methods.

A key question: SHOULD YOUR NOTES DUPLICATE THE TEXTBOOK AND LECTURE WORD FOR WORD? There are two major schools of thought here.

Some folks say note-taking can be a good way to recite the ideas in the book or lecture to yourself. If you can't explain something to yourself in your own words, that means you don't really know the material.

Others say you should be a human tape recorder and take down everything that is said. These folks believe that a lecture is not a time to think or meditate about what someone is saying, and that you can organize everything and begin to learn it after class when you start to organize and rewrite your notes.

NOTE: No matter which method of note-taking you use, keep these points in mind:

Be prepared to take notes before you get to class. If the instructor will be lecturing from certain pages in the book, look over the Table of Contents and the notes you have written in the book. This will set the road map in your mind. Also review your notes from the previous class.

Read aloud all captions, headings, italicized or boldfaced words, and key words that you have identified in the printed material three times before the lecture or class. This allows you to get the sound of the words in your head, and is especially important if the subject is technical or uses lots of jargon. Examples: onomatopoeia (English composition), osmosis (biology), res ipsa loquitur (law), claustrophobic (psychology). Even if you are pronouncing the word wrong, you may recognize it when the lecturer mentions it.

Don't forget your notebook and a pen, preferably in erasable ink. I suggest keeping notes from different classes in different spiral binders, i.e one for each class. That way, if you lose a binder, you won't lose your notes for every class. Erasable ink makes your notes just a little neater, since you don't have to scratch out.

Be as neat as possible, but don't be paranoid about neatness. Better an 'A' with sloppy notes that you understand than a 'C' with impeccable notes. Some people suggest writing on only one side of the page, with the flip side reserved for additions, changes, etc.

Always, always, take down everything the speaker says in the first five minutes and the last five minutes. The first few minutes are usually a summary of the last class or a preview of today's class. Sometimes they may even sneak in material that they know will be on the next test, so that the class can't complain that they never heard it.

The last few minutes may be a summary of today's class or a preview of the next one or an assignment you must complete.

Don't hurry. Incomplete notes usually come from trying to write too many details. If you miss something you feel is important, put a question mark at the end of the page and ask either the instructor or another student to explain it at the end of the class.

Your notes should not be excessively detailed, either. You are trying to record only the essential facts. The exception to this is when you are dealing with formulas, professional jargon or highly technical ideas in which every word has a specific meaning.

You should devise your own symbols and shorthand; abbreviate whenever possible. Most people use '+' instead of 'and', 're' instead or 'regarding', 'wrt' instead of 'with respect to', 'e.g' instead of 'for example', and so on. Many subjects also have their own abbreviations with which you will become familiar over time. You should also learn abbreviations the instructor typically uses.

Don't try to take cute notes. Use diagrams, charts, scribbles or whatever you need to make things clearer. I knew a brother who had a system. He wrote questions in red, the lecture in blue, and notes he had taken from the textbook in black. I don't know how effective his notes were, but at least they weren't dull.

Review your notes as soon as possible after taking them. This is really important if you don't have confidence in your note-taking ability. DON'T let you notes pile up with questions and incomplete thoughts. Otherwise, next week you won't be able to understand them.

NOTE-TAKING SYSTEMS

Most of us learned a classic note-taking method in elementary school. I'm talking about the Roman numeral outline form that looks like this:

    I.
       A.
       B.
          1.
          2.
             a.
             b.
    II.
       A.
       B.
          1.
          2.
             a.
             b.

and so on.

Why would they teach us all such a crappy system to be used for note-taking? It's fine for contracts, or for Tables of Contents, or for other documents which take time to prepare. For taking notes 'on the fly', while trying to listen and stay organized, it's lousy. You spend so much time trying to keep it organized that you miss most of what the instructor is saying. Also, this outline format is very inflexible.

According to the newer conventional methods, almost anything goes. Generally, the more imaginative your notes are (using different color pens, drawings, etc.) the more you should enjoy studying them and easier it is to recall them.

Some studying experts suggest taking textbook notes on one side of your notebook page and class notes on the other. This can work well because eventually you will have to integrate the class notes with the text ideas anyway.

All well and good. But let's evaluate a note-taking method that is the efficient, simplest, most direct, and most accurate I've seen. It even provides a method for you to check the accuracy of your notes.

THE HANAU SYSTEM OF NOTE-TAKING

This system, conceived by Laia Hanau and described in her book, The Study Game: How to Play and Win (4th Ed.), [Barnes and Noble, New York, 1979] is built on one basic idea.

That idea is that everything written or spoken is made up of only two elements: Statements (S) and Related Details (RD). Related details are only pieces of Proof, Information, or Example (PIE) about a statement.

Hanau says related details are used to control, direct, and guide the mind until it accepts or rejects what is said in the statement. She has developed an outline format that groups S's, and their RD's together. This is what it looks like:

FORMAT

        1 Statement (S)
          2 Related Detail (RD)
          3 Related Detail (RD)
          4 Related Detail (RD)

1 is the S; 2,3,4 are RD's. Notice that related details are indented under their statements.

Let's use this system to take notes on the following excerpts from a passage on firemaking which is taken from a U.S. Army field survival manual:

You need fire for warmth, for keeping dry, for signaling, for cooking, and for purifying water by boiling. Survival time is increased or decreased according to your ability to build a fire when and where you need it.

You should be able to build a fire under any condition of weather, if you have matches. For this reason, when operating in remote areas, always carry a supply in a waterproof case on your person.

SIZE, FUEL, LOCATION: Don't build your fire too big. Small fires are easier to control. Build a series of small fires in a circle around you in cold weather. They give more heat than one big fire. If your fire must be built on wet ground or snow, first build a platform of logs or stones. Protect your fire from the wind with a windbreak or reflector. These also concentrate the heat in the desired direction. Use standing dead trees and dry dead branches for fuel. The inside of fallen tree trunks will supply you with dry wood in wet weather. In treeless areas, rely on grasses, dried animal dung, animal fats, and coal, oil shale, or peat which may be exposed on the surface. If you are near the wreckage of an aircraft, use a mixture of gas and oil as fuel. Use kindling that burns readily to start your fire, such as small strips of dry wood, pine knots, bark, twigs, and palm leaves.

Using the Hanau system, your notes would look something like the next page.

The great thing about the Hanau system is that you can distinguish between the statements and the details by the position of the indentations. Let's try it here.

By the position of the related details, I know the passage has two important points to remember: (1) that I should always carry matches (line 1); and that there are a number of factors to consider in making the fire (line 8). Everything else in the passage is a related detail (RD) in some way to lines 1 and 8.

FORMAT   **YOUR NOTES**

FIREMAKING   FIREMAKING
1. _____   - Always carry matches in waterproof case on me in
                                                \remote areas
   2. _____   Fire is crucial to survival in the wild
     3. _____   - warmth
     4. _____   - signaling
     5. _____   - keeping dry
     6. _____   - cooking
     7. _____   - purifying water (boiling)

8. _____   - Factors to consider in firemaking:
  9. _____   - Size:
    10. __   - don't build too big
      11. __   - hard to control
    12. __   - build series of small fires
      13. __   - more heat than 1 big 1
14. _____   - Location:
    15. __   - platform, if wet or snow
      16. __   - windbreaker
    17. __   - concentrates heat
      18. __   - protects fire
19. _____   - Fuel:
    20. __   - in areas with trees
      21. __   - standing dead trees
      22. __   - dry dead branches
    23. __   - In treeless areas:
      24. __   - grasses
      25. __   - dry dung
      26. __   - coal, oil shale, peat
    27. __   - If crash
      28. __   - gas/oil mix
    '29. __   - Kindling to start fuel:
      30. __   - dry wood
      31. __   - pine knots
      32. __   - bark
      33. __   - twigs
      34. __   - palm leaves

Look at line 1. We see 1 RD below It; it is line 2, and it provides proof of why I should always carry matches. Keep in mind that an RD is only proof, information, or example about an S. Lines 3 through 7 give proof why firemaking is crucial. Thus they are RDs for line 2 only.

Note that line 2 is both a S and RD; if provides proof for the statement that I should always carry matches; it is also a statement of which is supported by other proofs in lines 3 through 7.

Look at lines 9, 14, and 19. By their indented position, you know that they are RDs for line 8. In plain English, that means that size, location and the type of fuel for the fire are factors to be considered in making a fire.

Look at lines 20, 23, and 27. They tell us what fuels may be needed to light the fire. Lines 29-34 describe the types of kindling which may be used to light the fuel.

Note again the indented positions. We can look and tell that use of a windbreaker (line 16) has nothing to do with the size of the fire (line 9) or with the type of fuel used (line 19). We know that the windbreaker is a factor in determining where the fire could be lit and that its functions are to concentrate heat (line 17) and protect the fire (line 18).

This type of note-taking that lets you see the interrelationships among ideas is important, and here's why.

Suppose you came to class and the instructor gave you a pop quiz consisting of one multiple choice question. Assume he allowed you to use your notes:

The primary purpose(s) of a windbreaker is/are to:
   a. control the fire
   b. to build a series of small fires
   c. to keep yourself dry
   d. all of the above
   e. a and c but not b
   f. none of the above

Look at the notes that were taken using the Hanau method and compare them with your usual notes. Would you have been able to determine that the correct answer was f?

To go any further into the Hanau system is beyond the scope of this book. Though I personally used only part of her system, I still highly recommend her book. There are other strategies which she outlines that may be very helpful to you.

THE CAREY-CHERRY METHOD OF NOTE-TAKING

There is another viable method of note-taking, but it is a high-risk strategy. That is depending on a classmate or classmates to do your notes for you.

For almost three years, I took graduate-level business courses while simultaneously taking law school classes. Sometimes the class time would conflict and I would have to miss a law lecture to attend a business class. It was then that I fell in love with Margaret Carey.

Margaret Carey was not only a good sister and a dedicated law student, but she was a human tape recorder. Her notes were usually organized and to the point; since she kept up with all the class reading assignments, she could tell what was important enough to write down. Since my notes were always lousy, I would register for classes with Margaret Carey in mind; if Margaret Carey was in that class section, I would get in that class by hook or crook. Margaret Carey's notes were an essential factor for me getting C's in law school classes I would otherwise have probably flunked.

The danger of such an approach should be clear to you. If you totally depend on somebody else to do your work for you, you effectively give him or her control of your academic life. My dependence on Margaret Carey went against the grain of the cardinal principle of academic life: Control your time and activities to the maximum extent possible. The best solution is to develop the best note-taking system possible for you and check with the instructors and your classmates on the items that you have missed.

SPEED READING

Contrary to popular belief, there is nothing mystical about speed reading. You don't have to take a $500 course to learn how to do it. The speed reading course I took as a second year law student in 1980 was sponsored by Student Government Association, was six hours long, and cost $15. I am still reaping the benefits from that course today.

Speed reading is merely the application of elementary skills used in conjunction with a small portion of your brain's amazing data processing potential. In summary, speed reading forces you to speed up or eliminate the 'voice' in your mind that pronounces the words in your head as your eyes scan the page, while at the same time, your eyes are forced to sweep the printed page. When used with a Table of Contents, chapter outlines, or study questions at the end of a chapter, speed reading becomes a powerful, indispensable tool.

OH, SAY, CAN YOU SEE?

This is not a stupid question. One reason some students have problems with reading is that they can't see well. If your eyes have difficulties focusing, if you get tired easily while reading, or you have vision-related problems, get a checkup. You may need glasses.

IS THERE A SECRET?

Nope.

Here's an example. As you are reading this page, a 'voice' in your head is slowly pronouncing each printed word. Your eye is probably focusing on only one word at a time, rather than on a streamofwordsinonesweep, or on a groupofwords thatcanbe puttogether acrossthepage. As a result of this mental and optical inefficiency, most people can read only as fast as they can talk. They move their eyes from one word to the next.

Your mind, however, moves at the speed of light and can retain data that you may not receive consciously.

Here is another simple example. If you own a videocassette recorder and set it to record programs automatically, the VCR will also record the commercials. When you look at the program, you will probably 'zap', or fast-forward the commercials till the program resumes on the tape. Most VCRs allow the viewer to see the commercial as it is zapped at three or four times the normal speed.

Because of the high costs of TV commercials, advertisers have been very concerned about zapping, because everyone thought that viewers would not remember the commercials. Recent research has found that this is not true. It makes no difference how fast the commercial is shown! The important thing is that the eyes see it because then the brain can perceive and remember it. These tests showed that people who watched zapped commercials at high speed remembered just as much as people who watched commercials at normal speed.

This confirms what is known about speed reading. Your brain can retain, in varying degrees, what your eyes can see. And with practice, your conscious mind will remember more in a shorter and shorter period of time.

That leads to this question: how can you increase you eye speed movement? Let your fingers do the walking, temporarily. As your eyes begin to sweep across the page, they will become too fast for your fingers.

Most peoples' eyes can follow fast-moving objects fairly easily and almost effortlessly. With practice, your eyes become disciplined and active rather than lazy, and are able to encompass more of the page in one glance.

Notice that as your eyes go faster across the page, the voice in your mind seems to accelerate itself by 'talking' faster. In fact your mind can always 'speak' faster than your mouth because your lips and tongue aren't involved. Incidently, if you are a person who pronounces words to himself or you move your lips while reading, those are habits that must be broken. You can do this while biting your tongue, literally, while reading until the habit is broken.

This is the essence of speed reading: increased active, effective comprehension through rapid eye movement and high concentration. Now let's see how speed reading can be used with other clues

to increase your retention of knowledge. An excellent source for specific techniques of speed reading is <u>Breakthrough Rapid Reading</u>, by
Peter Kump (Parker Publishing, West Nyack, NY, 1979).

SAVING TIME

True efficiency, to me, is finding the shortest, easiest way to
accomplish your goal. So many times the shortcuts that we can use
are staring us in the face, but we do not recognize them. Summaries
(Tables of Contents, chapter outlines, commercial outlines of the subject, Cliff Notes™, etc.), key words, and study questions are crucial
components of true scholastic efficiency. They are always readily
available for your use.

COMMERCIAL OUTLINES AND SUMMARIES

In most high school English Literature classes, students are
assigned a book or two to read at some time during the grading period. Almost everybody would go out and buy Cliff Notes™ or some
other commercial outline that summarized what the book was all
about. Usually folks would read the outline rather than reading the
book.

I strongly suggest that you purchase such an outline, if one is
available for your class textbook. If you are in a class that may have
mandatory outside reading assignments, see if you can find a store-
bought outline for these assignment.

Bear in mind, however, that reading a commercial outline is no
substitute for reading the stuff yourself. It only serves to start your
juices flowing. You'd be crazy to go into a lecture after merely reading the outline, because you probably would not be able to answer
any detailed questions the instructor may shoot at you. Rely on a
commercial outline as the basis for class discussion only as a last
resort. But use it as a road map to help you tie the big picture of the
course together.

PREFACES, FOREWORDS, INTRODUCTIONS

Almost every book has at least one of these in the front of the book. Almost everybody ignores these pages, which can be helpful to you.

The foreword is usually a pitch for the book written by someone other than the author. Occasionally, this may help you put the book in perspective by giving you an idea of what someone else thought of the book. The preface and the introduction are pretty much the same thing. Usually they give the reasons why and how the author has written the book. This can be helpful because it gives some idea of how the book is organized and the topics that the author considers to be important.

TABLE OF CONTENTS

Every textbook is developed from an outline or a logical list of topics that the book's author wants to cover. Usually this outline becomes the book's Table of Contents (we'll call it the TC from now on). The TC of your textbook is the most important element of both efficiency and test preparation, for a number of reasons.

First, the TC gives you the broad general overview of the whole course. If your instructor only uses one textbook, you know exactly what materials he or she will cover from Day One of the course.

Second, you can look at the TC as the instructor covers the material as the days go by and see where the subject you are currently studying fits in with the 'big picture'.

Third, you have a model on which to prepare your study outline of the course to prepare you for the exams. More on that later in this chapter.

Fourth, you may be able to estimate how much importance the author places on each subject by roughly estimating how much of the book is devoted to each subject.

The TC is an important aspect of speed reading because a quick reading of the TC plants key words and concepts in your mind even before you start reading the material. The TC prepares your mind to receive the information more easily, because the information will not be exactly 'new' to you. It gives you a good mental jump on the material you are about to read, because you are not reading blindly. You are reading actively, with an idea of reaching a specific destination that the author has in mind.

KEY WORDS

What are key words? They are words used by the author that tells you what the paragraph, chapter, or book is all about. For example the key words in the title of this book are 'academic excellence'. That will clue you that this book probably concerns itself with how to succeed in school.

How do you recognize key words? Very often they are nouns that name things, or are verbs that call for action. When you are reading through the TC or through the chapter outline that some authors follow in the text, you can mentally note the key words. There are even key words in every paragraph that you can also note that will tell you in a nutshell what that paragraph is all about. Usually the key words are found in the first sentence of every paragraph, which is also called the 'topic sentence'. To see if that is true, scan the first sentence of every paragraph of this page.

Key words may also be words you don't know. They may be important. They may be words that are familiar to you but may have a different meaning. For example, the word elastic has a different meaning when you are in home economics class as compared to a microeconomics class. You can get a jump by looking up all unfamiliar words in either the textbook's glossary or in a special dictionary (for law, medicine, math, etc.).

Study questions which are found at the end of the chapters in some books can also give you a jump on the material. They serve the same purpose as key words; that is, to preview the material you will be reading. Study questions are even better, because they pinpoint the areas that the author feels are the most important in the chapter.

Note, however, that the study questions may not emphasize what the instructor thinks is important. You should use the study questions only as a help which will help give you an introduction to the material.

SPEED READING TECHNIQUE: AN APPLICATION

Here is a suggested format for using speed reading and key word techniques to your advantage. Feel free to tinker with this and customize it to your own needs and abilities.

1. Read the Summary of Contents (if applicable). In books with 500 pages or more, the Table of Contents is so long that it is usually summarized. This summary is called the Summary of Contents, and will be listed in the front of the book before the Table of Contents. If the book does have a Summary of Contents, read it first. If there is no Summary of Contents, proceed to the next step.

2. Read the Table of Contents carefully. Notice the way the chapters are broken down; chronologically, by subject, from general to specific, etc. Get a good mental picture of where your reading assignment fits in with the rest of the topics.

3. Read the Preface and Introduction. Sometimes they give reasons why the book is organized as it is, as well as the assumptions on which the book is based.

4. Go to the reading assignment itself. Read the Chapter Outline carefully, if one is there. If not, read the section heading, and subheadings throughout the reading assignment. If there is no Chapter Outline and no section heading, throw the book away. (Just kidding.) But seriously, go to the next step.

5. Read the Study or Discussion Questions at the end of the chapter.

6. Read the first sentence of every paragraph of the assignment.

7. Read the reading assignment as fast as you comfortably can. At this point, you are reading simply to familiarize yourself with the material. Remember to detach your conscious mind from the material. Just let the words flow across your eyes and into your mind.

8. Read it again, at a slower rate of speed. Things should start to make sense when you get close to the end of the assignment.

9. Read it a third time, this time for comprehension. Look for key words and underline them in pencil (so that you can sell the book back if necessary). Make notes on the side of the page, if that's helpful.

Why, you ask, should an assignment be read three times? Won't it take longer than reading it once and taking notes the first time? Well, as usual, there is a method to the madness.

THE PRINCIPLE OF 'FIRST AND LAST': HOW TO USE BREAKS TO YOUR ADVANTAGE

Experience has shown that the mind has a tendency to remember things at the beginning and at the end of a series of events. Whatever happens in the middle has a tendency to fade from memory, because concentration seems to peak at the beginning and the end of whatever time period is involved.

This sounds complicated, but it's really not. Let's apply this to reading and studying.

Suppose that a reading assignment that you have been given will take approximately two hours to complete, using the usual technique of reading it just once and trying to take notes.

Even when you use that conventional technique, it is better to split the two-hour period into 'bursts' of 10, 20, or 30 minutes each with one or two-minute stretch breaks, rather than to go two hours continuously.

EXAMPLE:

_____ 2 HOURS _____

Remember the principle of 'first and last'. If you read this way, your mind may only remember the first 10 minutes and the last 10 minutes. Everything in between will probably be hazy.

BUT:

————30 min.————30 min.————30 min.————30 min.————

If you read this way, your mind will remember better, because the time between the first part of your study period and the last part of the period is shorter. So your comprehension will be better by studying in 'bursts' rather than continuously. This also serves to break up the monotony of the assignment, especially if it's in a subject you don't like or is highly technical.

Now, let's apply the 'first and last' principle to my suggested method of reading an assignment.

Note that by the time you will have finished the assignment, you have read the key words and concepts three to six times. This is important, because your mind responds to repetition. You can believe that by the third time, you have a good grasp of the points that the author is trying to get across.

At first glance, this may seem like a lot of work. It is not, when you consider what you have been able to accomplish. For one thing, you have a much better knowledge of the material now than you would have had if you had just plunged into it. And because you have read in bursts rather than continuously, your comprehension and retention of the stuff you have read will be much greater than it would have been. You have an idea of where the instructor is going. Additionally, you are ready to <u>outline</u> the assignment for the exam, if you so desire.

UNDERLINING/HIGHLIGHTING

Underlining key words, or highlighting them with a marker can be very helpful for review purposes. But it does no good if you underline the whole book! The idea is to have only the key words stand out. Once they do stand out, you can go back to the textbook and review the highlighted sections. If they buzz your brain into action when you see them, you are doing well and your preparation process is beginning to bear fruit.

Some folks believe it is better to underline or highlight what you don't know, rather than what you do know. I am of the opinion that you highlight both, so that you can get a summary of what is written at a glance. Of course, use whatever works best for you.

Underlining in pencil is better because you really don't know what is important until you have had a chance to begin an outline that puts your class notes and text together. If you underline the wrong thing, you can just erase it. Highlighting, however, is permanent and irrevocable. Also, if you decide to drop the class later, you can get more for the book if there are no permanent marks on it.

TAKING NOTES IN A BOOK

Your book can become more useful to you if you learn how to take notes in it. If you are using my suggestion of reading the material three times, you should take notes in the book on the last repetition, when your reading speed is the slowest and most deliberate.

Again, there are no standard rules for this. You should experiment and use the best method that works for you. Here are some suggestions that you should consider.

Get the overall meaning of the passage before you take notes on it. Just like in everything else, you need a mental road map. You should get this on the first two times you go over the material.

If the author has used an outline system in writing the book, use it to your advantage. Most books are put together logically, like this one, in which a main idea is given and related details are used to support it. Some are put together in an outline form in which the author uses letters and numbers to make it easier to understand.

Create a simple, practical system of notations and stick to them.

EXAMPLES:
Underlining/highlighting: used to indicate the "meat" of the passage, i.e the main ideas. Quick glances at underlined or highlighted passages should give you a very quick, short review of what is important.

0 Circle around a word: indicates jargon, or a special word used that may not be known or used in everyday language.

E in the margin: used to indicate information possibly used in an exam.

$\underline{[\;]},\underline{(\;)},\underline{\backslash\;/}$: can be used to indicate an important idea or group of ideas. You can underline the key words within the passage for greater clarity.

$\underline{?}$: Indicates something you don't understand.

$\underline{!}$: Indicates something that comes as a surprise, or is completely different from what you understand about the subject.

$\underline{1,2,3,4}$: Indicates a series of facts, ideas, etc. that are important.

OUTLINING/SUMMARIZING: THE TRUE SECRET OF SUCCESS

Up to this point, we have discussed various component skills that will make you a better and more efficient student. Now we shall put all of those skills together to produce what I consider to be the single most important document in the whole study process: the <u>OUTLINE</u>.

The outline is quite simply an organized, logical summary of the whole course. It puts together class notes, textbook principles, questions and answers, examples of problems and their solutions, and other helpful information about the instructor, the course, or the test.

If your outline is properly prepared, you should not have to refer to class notes or the textbook during exam preparation. Your outline will be the basis of your studying; all you should be doing is working possible test problems and writing sample answers.

WHEN DO I BEGIN MY OUTLINE?

The best time to begin putting together an outline is immediately after class, if you have blocked off the time. The most effective outlines are the ones that include all of the things that you have studied in class. Naturally, the material is still fresh in your mind (hopefully) right after you leave the lecture.

Many students get into the practice of rewriting their notes immediately after the class, and for good reason. Usually your notes are somewhat disjointed because you are writing, thinking, and trying to pay attention to the lecture simultaneously. Rewriting them immediately also reinforces the lecture and helps you think of questions you may have later.

Rewriting immediately is also more efficient. Let's suppose your school is on the semester system. You are taking 15 hours (five classes, three times per week). In each lecture you take two to three pages of notes, three times per week. That's at least 30-35 pages of notes per week; that adds up to at least 450 pages of notes that you must review over the course of a 15-week semester during finals, if the final is cumulative.

Need I say more?

Another key question: SHOULD I WRITE IN MY OWN WORDS? As with other topics, there are different schools of thought.

Some folks feel that you are taking a serious risk by putting ANY-THING in your own words, which is called paraphrasing, because you run the serious risk of learning the wrong information, unless you have a way of checking to see if your paraphrasing is correct.

Others believe that paraphrasing is indispensable, and that you never really learn anything without being able to accurately explain it in your own words.

My experience falls more in the latter category. For me, copying verbatim what somebody else says wouldn't cut it. You must make the material yours, and you do this by rewriting and explaining it in a different way. This is true even if you are borrowing very heavily from somebody else's outline or notes, as I often did.

Be careful, however, that you can use the 'jargon' of the class correctly and that you can explain definitions in the way that the instructor wants. This is particularly true in areas where a lot of technical language or jargon is used, such as biology or computers. To me, the biggest frustration in academia is to organize and study diligently, and still flunk a test. You knew the answers, but couldn't understand what the instructor was looking for, since you couldn't use his own language.

You can check yourself by meeting with the instructor, as I discuss in the next chapter, by study groups, and by asking questions after class to determine if your version of what was said is correct.

HOW TO MAKE A GOOD OUTLINE

Above all, an outline is always LOGICAL. It should make sense. Other than that, there are no hard and fast rules.

Some people are disciplined enough to rewrite notes daily and incorporate all of the necessary sources in their notes. Most students don't do this, which means they will, at some point in time, be faced with organizing a mass of material.

The Hanau system, discussed previously, is a great way of organizing an outline because it follows a simple logical format. Whether you use the Hanau system or your own, the following suggestions will be helpful:

1. <u>Gather all the sources you need: textbook, notes, reference books, etc</u>. If you missed any class notes, you should copy them from a classmate. Also, make sure you have three to four hours of uninterrupted time. Interruptions interfere with the concentrated analytic process so vital to your success.

2. <u>Look first at the course syllabus,</u> if your instructor has given you one, to see how your outline should be structured. Then look to the TC and compare it with the syllabus. If there is no syllabus, use the TC as your guide.

If the instructor has skipped around, it may be because there may have been a limited amount of time to cover a lot of academic ground. Ask the instructor if you will be responsible for materials that may not be on the syllabus, but that he may have skipped over according to the TC. This is not a dumb question. Don't take anything for granted!

3. <u>Divide by topics as done in either the TC or the course syllabus</u>. This makes it easier because the lectures will usually follow either one or the other. Another important tactic is to use categories and classifications that you have noticed in your subject.

Example: Look at our firemaking example as formatted on page 67. One portion of the passage was conveniently categorized as 'factors to consider' in firemaking, which makes it easier to learn.

4. Incorporate the textbook and the class notes together in the same section. Usually the lecture will explain or amplify the text. Don't have one outline of class notes and another for the textbook. Putting them together forces you to look from one to another in an effort to find similarities. Sometimes you may find disagreement; if so, check your notes with someone else or ask the instructor what he or she said.

5. Make diagrams or pictures to help make things clearer to you. Many times instructors will draw diagrams and charts that explain a point. Use them in your outline. An issue graph or a flow chart may make things much more understandable. Making pictures also forces you to think as you draw.

6. Include all in-class problems in the outline. Many times instructors will ask the class a question or pose a hypothetical problem, then call on students to solve it. In some classes, there is not much lecturing done. For example in law school, students learn the law, are given factual problems in class, then argue with each other about why the result logically should be either this or that. The instructor usually only guides the discussion. This is called the Socratic method of study.

Regardless of whether the class is lecture or Socratic, many of the problems and questions instructors ask have a way of coming back to haunt students on exams. Sometimes the instructor will give the answer in class exactly as he would want it back on a test. Other times, they may tell you how the problem should be analyzed, but not give you the conclusion or their answer. But even that is OK, because you know where the teacher is coming from. Also, you have an opportunity to find the answer, if there is one, at home rather than at test time. Isn't that wonderful?

7. Don't make your outline too cute. You are not writing a masterpiece. An outline is meant to be marked up, underlined, highlighted, and scratched out as you study it. Don't be compulsive about neatness.

8. <u>Make notes of any questions you may have</u>. Sometimes further study will answer the question, sometimes not. If not, ask the instructor.

9. <u>Share the outline with a classmate</u>. Assuming they can understand it, this will provide valuable input. You may misunderstand something that is reflected in the outline that a classmate may catch.

MEMORY SYSTEMS

Once you have summarized all the stuff you are responsible for learning, the next task is to organize it in a way that your mind can easily recall. The easiest way is with a memory system of your own or one that you can easily learn.

If you have a photographic memory and can memorize lists, numbers, formulas or concepts with no trouble, more power to you. Your own system, whatever it is, is getting you over big-time.

LORAYNE 'LINK AND PEG' METHOD

But if you are a mere mortal like the rest of us and must work at memorization, I strongly suggest you immediately check out from your nearest library or purchase <u>How to Develop A Super Power Memory</u> by Harry Lorayne (New American Library, 1974).

Lorayne, a memory expert who routinely memorizes phone books in his spare time, believes that there is no such thing as a poor memory-only an untrained one. Anyone can be trained to remember whatever he or she wants to remember.

Why do our memories seem to be so bad? Here are a few of the most common reasons:

<u>We never remembered in the first place</u>. Many times we never have any original awareness of what it was we forgot. For example, I am constantly looking for my car keys because I always 'forget' where I put them. The real reason I'm always looking for them is because I never noticed where I put them. Those minutes wasted are the price

paid for inattention to a 'detail' that is important.

Memory, awareness, and observation go hand in hand. It is difficult, if not impossible, to remember something you don't want to
remember or are not interested in remembering.

Our minds have become lazy from disuse. The mind is like a mus-
cle. It must be used constantly to function at its best. The memory is
the same way. A German psychologist discovered that people forget
almost three-fourths of what they have learned one hour after they
have learned it; after 24 hours, almost 85% is forgotten.

So many of us write things down because we are too lazy to take
the effort to remember them. As Lorayne says, "your handwriting will
improve, or the speed of your writing might improve, but your memory will get worse through neglect and non-use."

The Pygmalion effect. This is the proper name given for what is
also known as a 'self-fulfilling prophesy.' That's when we say to ourselves, "I'm never gonna remember all this when I take the test." Subconsciously, the mind starts to believe that; the memory fails come test
time, and we tell ourselves, "I knew I wouldn't remember."

This is a problem of self-confidence, and we have discussed that
at the beginning of this book. The most important thing is to eliminate
all negative thoughts about your ability to accomplish any academic
goal you have set.

Lorayne uses the Link method to remember concepts, ideas,
names, items, etc. Like most great ideas, it is very simple.

Associate, or link, each thing you want to remember with a picture in your mind. The more ridiculous and the illogical the picture is,
the better. And when you think of one thing, you will automatically
think of the other. Here's a simple example using our firemaking passage again.

We have to remember a number of things: why carry matches
and factors to consider in firemaking.

CARRYING MATCHES: I see in my mind a giant MATCH, wearing a raincoat, carrying me and setting me down before a FIRE. All around I see thousands of other matches WARMing themselves and keeping DRY in front of a fire. One is bent over warming his hands. As I look at the fire, I see my instructor being COOKED in a pot of BOILING WATER as one match spoons broth over his head.

So far, I have used the Links to remember that I should <u>carry matches</u> in a waterproof case on my person at all times, because the fire is crucial to my survival, primarily for <u>warming</u>, <u>keeping dry</u>, <u>cooking</u>, and <u>boiling water</u>.

FACTORS IN FIREMAKING: As my professor is being boiled, he is screaming FACTS at the top of his lungs. "Twelve inches equals one foot! Three feet equals one yard!" Suddenly, out of nowhere, a 7-foot tall lit match (BIG FIRE) confronts the professor, who has a tape measure measuring the big fire's SIZE. He is defended by thousands of SMALL lit matches (FIRES), who blow the big match out. Then, a LOCOmotive comes within 1 inch of the professor. The train stops and puts the professor on a PLATFORM, as thousands of small matches begin to dance around the pot, all wearing WINDBREAKERS, since it is SNOWING, and holding umbrellas on their heads (PROTECTION). Meantime, Glen Rice, a Miami HEAT pro basketball player I recognize, is playing the game show CONCENTRATION next to the small fires in windbreakers holding umbrellas.

I can now remember that two <u>fact</u>ors of firemaking includes <u>size</u> of the fire, with <u>small fires</u> preferable to <u>big fires</u>. Theother factor, <u>loc</u>ation, means placing the fire on a <u>platform</u> if it <u>snows</u> or rains, and that a <u>windbreaker</u> should be used for <u>heat</u> <u>concentration</u> and <u>protection</u>.

The beautiful thing about the Link system is that if you can use things that are meaningful only to you; faces, situations, words, people, etc. Also, if you somehow forget a word, you can think about another word in the Link and the picture will pop up in your mind. If you have the picture fixed in your head the "missing Link" will be there.

Example: suppose all I remember is the word `location'. If the picture is fixed in my mind, I see the train, then the platform, then the snow and the little fires dancing in windbreakers and umbrellas.

The Link method also works backward and forward. Try it with our example and see.

Here are the keys to establishing vivid Links in your mind:

Picture the items out of proportion. In my example, the seven-foot match was so big that it was easy to remember.

Picture the words in action. Because of our perverse minds, it is easier to remember strange kinds of events, such as a match wearing a condom for protection, rather than an umbrella. But since it's your Link, nobody need know what you are thinking.

Exaggerate the amounts of items. In our example, we see thousands of little matches overwhelming the single big match and warming themselves around the fire.

Substitute items. We didn't use substitution in our example, so let me give you another quick one. Suppose you were trying to link nail and typewriter. Instead of seeing typing keys, you could visualize your fingers typing on nails on the typewriter.

Lorayne also has a system for remembering numbers called the Peg method. I refer you to his book for further details.

ANOTHER MEMORY METHOD: UNITS OF FOUR OR LESS

Another method, again outlined in the Hanau book, is to categorize and reorganize the list of items to remember so that they are always in units of four or less. For some reason, the mind seems to remember things better when they are four or less.

Again, using our firemaking example, on page 67, note that there are six types of fuel (lines 21, 22, 24, 25, 26, 28) in three categories (lines 20, 23, 27). See if you can categorize them in units of four or less. Then, try learning the whole list of six, by category, using the Link system.

ANOTHER MEMORY METHOD: MNEMONICS

A mnemonic (pronounce new-MON-ic) device is simply a memory trick which uses letters in a word or sentence. Each letter stands for the word you actually want to remember. For example, the word HOMES was used when I was in my elementary school geography class to remember the five Great Lakes: Huron, Ontario, Michigan, Erie, Superior. In music, a mnemonic is Every Good Boy Deserves Fudge; the letters represent the musical notes on a treble clef of a musical staff. See if you can do the same thing for our firemaking example.

When using this method, remember that the mnemonic does not have to be a recognizable word. It can be any collection of letters that you can remember. Or it can be a sentence. For example, the mnemonic I made for the two main factors in our firemaking story is the good ship SS LPSWHCP pronounced Lap-Swee-Hiccup. The letters represent Size: Small. Location:Platform if Snow;Windbreaker for Heat Concentration and Protection. If you can remember the letters, you can remember the words they represent.

Regardless of the system used, we can summarize and mention additional factors that will lead to improving your memory.

Learn the right information. Seems simple enough, but it must be said. Make sure that what you are attempting to memorize is correct!

Understand what you are trying to memorize. Otherwise it means nothing. You won't be able to explain it, and therefore you haven't learned it. This is especially true of formulas. If you just know the symbols, that does you no good. You should know the concepts and be able to tell your instructor what makes the formula fit together.

Pay attention to 'small' details. Begin to notice things about your environment. Consider using the Link system just for practice to remember them.

Recite the items you have memorized aloud. Practice, practice, practice will fix the Links in your mind, if you use the system.

Use your 'down time' to go over the Links. When you are in the bathroom, riding to school, or eating alone, you can use this time to improve your recall.

Be creative. After all, who is in your head but you? Your imagination is as broad or as limited as you want it to be.

Continue to have confidence that you can remember whatever you want to or have to in order to be successful.

ENGLISH AND WRITING SKILLS

The English language is my enemy...

> (R)acism is inherent in the English language because the language is an historic expression of the experience of a people; that racism, which is the belief that one group is superior to the other and has the right to set the standards for the other, is still one of the main spiritual policies of our country as expressed in the educational process.

Ossie Davis, The Black Language
Reader: R.H. Bentley, S.D. Crawford
(eds.): Scott, Foresman & Co.,1973

No other skill you will learn in elementary school will serve you better than good basic English grammatical and writing skills. Almost every day in newspapers and magazines, you can read about the alarming erosion of basic writing and language skills in this country.

No sector of American society is unaffected. Businessmen with master's degrees cannot write a decent two-page report. Secretaries can't spell or make sentence subjects agree with the verbs. Students can't pass essay exams. Lawyers can't write legal pleadings without pages and pages of errors.

This skills erosion has had an even more devastating effect on Black students because our writing skills were generally perceived to be poorer anyway, for a couple of good reasons. But before I get into the reasons, let me focus on the word <u>perceived</u>.

In doing research for this book, I was pleasantly surprised that linguists (people who study languages) are now saying that Black America has been one of the primary influences in making Standard American English the rich, descriptive, lively language that it is. Not only have we contributed new words to the country's vocabulary (jazz, nitty-gritty, ripoff, etc.), we have used our imagination to change the meaning of standard words (cool, cold, chill, bad, fresh, etc.)

Most modern linguists also agree that Black English has grammar, rules, and structure that are very different than Standard American English. Many also agree that Black English originated from West Africa's languages via the slave trade and expansion by Europe's ocean-sailing ships.

One of the most fascinating things I found out was many linguists believe that Blacks and their speech have had the greatest influence on the speech of Southern whites. Said one writer as cited in <u>Black English</u>, by J. H. Dillard (Random House, N.Y., 1972) :

> It must be confessed, to the shame of the white population of the South, that they perpetuate many of these pronunciations in common with their Negro dependents; and that, in many places, if one happened to be talking to a native with one's eyes shut, it would be impossible to say whether a Negro or white person were talking.
>
> at page 252

The point of this review is to get you to understand that the way Black folks speak is not wrong; it is not incorrect. It is just <u>different</u> from Standard English and should be recognized and taught as such. But America being the kind of country that it is, Black English is <u>perceived</u> as inferior. So are the Black people who speak it.

ARE YOU BILINGUAL?

Moses Malone, the basketball player, said he felt no need to take

English lessons because folks could understand what he was talking about. Most Black folks I know speak Black English well and folks can understand what they are saying. If they were given tests on Black English, they would pass with flying colors. It is the tests of Standard English that we seem to have problems with, for two reasons.

First: the tests just don't test things within our everyday experience, especially in tests that evaluate written and verbal Standard English, as I mentioned in the previous chapter.

As a born and bred Southerner, I speak with a pronounced drawl. There is no way that you can speak to me over the phone and not be able to tell that I am Black, if you know what I mean.

I speak at home with my Black family and friends in Black English and I am not ashamed of that. I am especially fond of splitting a verb every now and again. But I can switch to both speaking and writing Standard English as the need arises.

Have you ever tried to write the way most Black folks speak, exactly as we sound, with slang and everything? For example, this is what I sound like at home:

> When um in da coatroom tryin' a case befo a jury, ah wont dem jurors focusin' in own me an not muh gramma. Even dough ah got a Southern drawl, ah kin switch the lingo whenever ah wonna.

Let's translate and correct that to Standard English, as if I were telling this to an audience of fellow attorneys:

> When I'm in the courtroom trying a case before a jury, I want those jurors focusing on me and not on my grammar. Even though I have a Southern drawl, I can switch languages whenever I wish.

Now suppose you live in an environment where everybody speaks non-standard English all day long. You speak it. Your friends and family speak it. Nobody tells you there's anything 'wrong' with the way you speak. And if you try to speak like the folks on television, your friends and family start to look at you funny because you are "talking proper" or "talking white" and selling out to the white folks.

If you don't read much, you never get a chance to see how the Standard English words are spelled. You aren't particularly interested in whether your subject agrees with your verb. Your teacher doesn't really impress upon you the importance of learning standard English and the effect it will have on your whole life.

Then, somebody decides to test your standard English skills in preparation for passing a class, or being promoted, or graduating from high school, or entering college, or getting a job. How well do you think you would do?

That brings us to the second reason our written and verbal skills are perceived to be poor: underdeveloped or underdeveloped reading, writing, and vocabulary abilities in STANDARD English. This is especially noticeable on tests which have vocabulary or essay components.

Yet, some Black academicians are apologists. They point to discrimination and social factors as the reasons for our poor performance, which is true. They say there is nothing wrong with 'Black English', which is also true. But why aren't folks telling the truth to young Black students?

The truth is splitting verbs and disregarding grammar will hurt you in school and it will kill you in the corporate environment. It is one thing to speak a different language by choice. It is another to speak the language because you don't know anything else. I believe if you knew better, you would do better.

The Black educational establishment and Black parents are failing Black children, Blacks generally, and the country itself by not attacking the problem. There should be a mandatory course with the sole aim of making Black students bilingual. And if you didn't get those skills from elementary school to high school you'd better do your best to get them now.

Another truth is that many employers will not tell you to take speech or writing courses. He or she will just fire you and leave you scratching your head, "Why?" In fact, at this writing, I am handling an employment discrimination case which revolves around the inability of two Black employees to 'properly communicate to customers and managers' over the phone. Hell, I could understand both perfectly.

Notice, however, that switching languages implies a knowledge of the other language. You can't switch from English to Spanish if you don't know Spanish; similarly, you can't switch from Black English to Standard English if you don't know Standard English.

If you have to learn Standard English as if it was a second language, then do it. If you want to learn Standard English in order to correct what you feel is an incorrect and inferior language used in the Black community, fine with me. Whatever your attitude, learn how to speak it and write it correctly.

Let me give you another reason you should learn Standard English. (For some of you less enlightened brothers and sisters, this may be the most important reason.)

The business world will pay you for it! There are two basic factors why.

One is strictly market value. Because competent writers are few these days, you have a skill that is in demand.

The other factor is because of lower expectations that whites have of an 'athletically superior/intellectually inferior' Black race. Therefore, when a Black person has a particular skill that other Blacks seem not to have, that person becomes more valuable.

If you are at all unsure of your grammar skill, get help. Take remedial classes, study on your own, do whatever is necessary to improve your skills.

I also suggest reading as much as you can about everything, if you have not already developed a habit of reading. Reading helps to build your vocabulary as well as increase your general knowledge.

Get into the habit of looking words up in the dictionary or in a thesaurus, which is a dictionary listing words that mean the same thing. Browse through them during lunch or dinner or during your other 'down times': waiting for the bus, between classes, etc. It is really more fun than it sounds. It's fascinating to understand what a rich language English is. Also, you can shock the brothers and sisters on the 'set' when you tell them that you have grown weary of the quotidian drabness of school life and that you look forward to a less pedestrian lifestyle in the near future. (Translation: You are tired of school, and look forward to living a great life after graduation.)

There are many books on vocabulary and English that can help you, some of which are in the List of References of this book.

WHY YOU SHOULD LEARN HOW TO TYPE

As I dust off my memories about high school, I seem to remember that it was OK to turn in a hand-written report.

Well, forget it in college, at least most of the time. You will be responsible for presenting typewritten reports to instructors, and they won't accept excuses. Being able to type is a big advantage because you don't have to spend money on typists, especially if you must turn in two or three drafts of major papers.

Having typing skills enables you to knock out short papers at the last minute, if necessary. It also improves your ability to work with computer keyboards with speed and accuracy. If you are in engineering, math, computer science, journalism, or any other major that is computer terminal-intensive, you need to know how to type. In fact, almost every field of knowledge these days is using computers. Hunting for and pecking the keys slows you down.

If you don't know how to type, consider taking a typing course during the summer break or at night. The small investment will last a lifetime. If you can type, consider buying or leasing a home computer with good word processing software, a dedicated word processor, or a good typewriter with an electronic 'spelling checker' or memory. The ability to rewrite and store notes and outlines in these devices is absolutely fabulous.

The computer world has entered the fourth generation of 'laptop' computers. It is now possible to have the text of this entire book and more in a computer that is smaller than a portable typewriter for about $2000, including a budget printer.

It is my belief that the laptop will revolutionize academics by raising the expectations of the written performance of all students. Since computers can check spelling, syntax, and grammar (including subject-verb agreement and verb tense, in some cases), there won't be excuses for bad writing much longer. Since laptops and printers are getting smaller and cheaper, more and more students (and instructors) are taking advantage of the technology.

Soon, laptops may be as commonplace in high school and college as calculators are in your math class, with predictable effects on Black students who are not prepared for the change. Any problems you already have with grammar will become even more evident.

LIBRARY SKILLS

The library can be a gold mine if you know how to use it. Some libraries file old tests by class or instructor or both. Additionally, sometimes an instructor will use another textbook as his primary reference in class discussion. He or she may take questions directly from that book.

Hopefully you were given a guided tour of your school's library during freshman orientation. If not, go on a guided tour or either get a map and wander around the place yourself. Talk to a librarian who can give you an idea of any special capabilities the library may have: computerized research, computers that may be available for student use, video and audiotapes, special book collections, signing up for study carrels, loan procedures with out-of-town libraries, etc.

As you use the library for various term papers and research projects, your research skills will increase and sharpen. If you feel like you are totally lost the first few times, don't worry about it. It'll get better.

HOW I SPENT MY SUMMER VACATION

Here's an excellent example of how a well-prepared outline can prepare you for almost any test.

During the summer of 1983, I spent seven weeks in Notasulga, AL. at the home of my brother Glenn, who was gone for the summer after finishing his second year of veterinary school at Tuskegee Institute (now Tuskegee University). There I studied for the Florida Bar exam. During that seven-week period of time, I was faced with the formidable task of mastering the laws of Property, Evidence, the U.S. and Florida Constitutions, Wills, Trusts, Torts, U.S and Florida Criminal Law and Procedure, Contracts, Florida Rules of Civil Procedure, and Business Entities. One course I had never studied in law school; others I had not studied or looked at in four years.

The test itself was a monster, but it sure could have been worse. (Now it IS worse because they have added more subjects.) It was 12 hours spread out over two days. The first day we would have 6 hours to answer 200 multiple choice questions, some of which were the toughest I had ever seen. These would cover six subjects. The second day it was another six hours of both multiple choice and essay questions. However, four of the six hours would cover only four subjects of the seven we were responsible for knowing. Therefore, three of the subjects I would study would not even be on the exam. What a sadistic twist!

I was in trouble and I knew it. An organized bar review course cost $500 at that time, but people who had successfully passed the exam told me that taking the whole course was a waste of money. They said that the summaries prepared for the courses were sufficient, if I could discipline myself to study for the test. One good friend, David Self, offered to give me his old materials, which were two years old and possibly out of date.

I am a cheap guy. I took the materials, hoping that little had changed in the law in only two years. I packed my car with clothes, textbooks, casebooks, old class outlines, commercial outlines, class notes, sample test questions, and anything else I could get my hands on and took off from Daytona Beach, FL for Notasulga, AL.

After clearing the place of ticks, fleas, roaches and snakes (I actually shot a rattlesnake in the living room under a chair), I gathered all of my books and papers on the living room table. Immediately depression and self-doubt set in. This is crazy, I thought. I can't do this. It's too much. It's too late. I should have started this months ago. My materials are dated. There's nobody to study with. I don't know where to start. I'm gonna flunk it. Then everybody's gonna know I couldn't pass the Bar exam.

This went on for what seemed to be hours. Finally, I was able to get ahold of myself. I recognized what I had been doing for what it was: I was laying the groundwork for my own failure by coming up with excuses I could make after I flunked the test. It was then that I decided that I would do whatever was necessary to pass the Florida Bar exam.

That was a crucial battle to win: the battle of my academic and personal self-confidence against self-condemnation for not studying sooner, and doubts about my ability to get the job done. But how to win the war? The first thing I did was go through the same pre-season conditioning technique that I have described to you here, beginning with a self-assessment.

POINT OF REFERENCE: I knew I could pass if I had a good plan. I knew that I had graduated from the state's best law school and that they had given me the basic knowledge to pass the test. I knew this test was tough, but that the University of Florida's JD/MBA was tougher.

I knew also that many of my Black classmates thought that there was outright discrimination on the test, that Blacks were somehow singled out for failure. I believed this on an emotional basis, but my logical mind told me this was just a rationalization. I decided that as long as I felt I had given it my best shot by preparing myself adequately, I wouldn't worry about alleged discrimination. The Lord would take care of that.

SUPPORT SYSTEMS: Good. My parents were behind me 110 percent; friends and family who knew where I was would often call and encourage me. My fraternity brothers on the Tuskegee campus would call about parties. My close cousins and friends were in Atlanta, a two-hour drive away.

STRESS REDUCTION: Crucial. My physical conditioning was fair because I had joined a health club in Daytona, but I didn't go regularly.

I decided to do Yoga stretching exercises in the morning and to run and exercise for an hour when it got cool in the evening. Weekends, barring any major problems, would be reserved for hanging out in Atlanta.

MY SELF-ASSESSMENT: Strong writing and organizational skills. Writing under deadline pressure was no problem. No need to brush up on grammatical skills. Weak in multiple choice skills, since no multichoice tests in law school. Virtually no recall on some subjects; one major subject, Evidence, never taken in school. Memory systems, speed reading had not been used in a long time. Level of motivation high because of fear of failure, large ego. Discipline level low since graduation. Bottom line: I had become academically fat and lazy in just six months since graduation.

I made some important decisions. First, I picked out (a) the most important subject; (b) the toughest subject.

On the multichoice part of the exam, the law and rules of Evidence would be the priority. It was a mandatory subject; 40 of 200 questions would be Evidence questions, so I had to study it. Coincidentally, Evidence would be the toughest subject for me; I did not take Evidence in law school. Since I had no idea of what the subject was about, I had to allot extra time to study it.

Second, I must restore and improve my memory and speed reading skills. There was too much stuff to read in a short period of time to fiddle around. Also, I could not depend on myself to remember all the different principles of law without a memory system. I would not have time to fumble around during the exam because of a lack of knowledge of the basics.

Third, I must follow the same daily routine without major variation for the whole seven weeks. Here was the plan:

6am-7am	Yoga exercises, watch TODAY show, eat
7-12 noon	study w/ breaks as necessary
noon-1 pm	eat, go to town to pick up mail
1-5 pm	study w/ breaks as necessary
5-7 pm	run, shower, watch the news, eat
7-11 pm	study w/ breaks as necessary

11-midnight   light reading till sleepy
(no reading of anything remotely related to the law.)

Thursday nights: 'Cheers' and 'Hill Street Blues'.

Friday night-Sunday evening:
                              travel to Atlanta for partying,
                              visiting family, concerts, etc.

Fourth, I calculated that I must go through all the topics AT LEAST three times before they were firmly fixed in my mind. I decided I would prepare an outline of each subject. The last week would be reserved for test-taking.

I pulled out my calendar. Actually I had eight weeks and a few days till the test itself. The last two weeks included two days travel time back to Florida and the day before the test to spend cooling out and relaxing. I also knew that there was a weekend 'crash' course on the multiple choice portion approximately 8 days before the test. I decided to reserve that weekend in case I needed last-minute help.

The first day was spent reviewing principles of memory systems and speed reading. I re-read Harry Lorayne's book on memory. It had been indispensable to me in preparing for law school exams. Later on that day, I made out a study schedule for the eight weeks. The topics were grouped so that I could read a consistent amount of material every day.

It took four days of speed reading to get through the materials the first time. The second time took a week because I was reading to understand. But before I started reading the text, I would always read the TC to refamiliarize myself with the 'big picture'. So I had already used two weeks and had not written down anything, but the time was certainly not wasted. I could feel my mind beginning to slowly absorb the material.

At the beginning of the third week I was reading this stuff for the third time. This time I started outlining and summarizing what I was reading in my own words. If I had a question, I would look at some of the supplementary sources I had (other textbooks, class notes, etc.)

and would put that in the outline. Again, I could feel myself getting a better understanding of the law.

It took about four weeks to outline all the courses. I had now used six of the eight-plus weeks. After finishing all the outlines, I then summarized each outline and associated each important point to only one or two words. Thus, an Evidence study guide that was originally 108 pages long when I started studying six weeks ago was now less than one page. I then used the Link memory system to remember these key concepts.

This summarizing took about a week. I was now at the beginning of week seven of the eight. It was now showtime: time to take sample tests. I was beginning to feel the time pressure, so I canceled my weekend trips to Atlanta.

The magic number at that time on the Florida bar was 61% accuracy. I hardly came close to that number on the multiple choice questions the whole week. There were some gaping holes in my understanding that had to be plugged up, and I didn't have too much time to do it.

The sample questions had supplied the correct answers, but no analysis was given. My recall of the material was good, but I couldn't apply it to the multiple choice questions. I decided to take the multiple choice crash course when I got back to Florida. For now, I would concentrate on learning materials and writing sample essay answers.

To make a long story short: I went back to Florida, took the course, answered multiple choice questions the last weekend before the exam, took the exam, and passed it the first time, using 2-year-old borrowed materials, and the system described in this book.

My highest multichoice test scores came in the topic of Evidence, a subject I never studied in law school, but which I taught myself in six weeks.

THIS SYSTEM WORKS.

SUMMARY

GRADES ARE CRITICAL, and are 'weighted' toward your first year. **GET AHEAD EARLY;** you won't have to work so hard to keep your grades up.

Listening is a skill that must be learned. You must prepare to listen, restrain your emotions about the speaker, adjust to his/her speech patterns, concentrate, and filter.

Taping class lectures is a waste of time. If you have a good note-taking system, keep it. If your system is bad, consider using the Hanau system, or using the suggestions in this chapter.

Depending on someone else's notes is a viable strategy. However, you break a cardinal principle of academic life: **CONTROL YOUR TIME AND ACTIVITIES TO THE MAXIMUM EXTENT POSSIBLE.**

'Speed reading' is a skill you can learn and is accomplished by coordinating your eyes, hand and brain more effectively.

Commercial summaries and outlines of books can give you a better understanding of the 'big picture' of the assignment, book, or subject. Use them when possible.

Don't ignore prefaces, forewords, and introductions to books, which tell you why the book was written and how it is organized.

The Table of Contents of your course textbook can give you a broad overview of the course and can be used as a model for writing your own course outline.

Use key words in titles, topic sentences, and paragraphs to introduce your mind to the subject matter you will be reading. This will improve your comprehension and retention.

Develop a system to make notes (in pencil) directly in your textbook.

Make a comprehensive outline, including class notes, textbook notes, reference books, in-class problems, in preparation for an exam.

A memory system (units of four, mnemonics, or a Link/Peg-type) is effective in remembering facts, numbers, and formulas.

LEARN TO PROPERLY SPEAK AND WRITE THE ENGLISH LANGUAGE. If you have to study it like a foreign language, do so.

Take a typing course, if you have not already done so. This will improve your ability to work with computers and type your own term papers, etc.

Get very, very familiar with your school library.

If possible, meet the instructor personally before you sign up for class.

<u>CHAPTER FIVE</u>

THE MARATHON BEGINS

If you desire ease, forsake learning. If you desire learning, forsake ease. How can a man at ease acquire knowledge, and how can an earnest student enjoy ease?

Nagarjuna

You don't pay the price for your hard work; you enjoy the benefits. Life is tough, but if you're tough on yourself, life will be infinitely easier. When you do the things you ought to do when you ought to do them, the day will come when you can do the things you want to do when you want to do them.

Zig Ziglar

RUNNING TO WIN

You have done all the training that is necessary to increase your probability of academic success. You have learned all the skills necessary to give you the edge. Now it is time to put everything into operation.

ESTABLISH A DAILY ROUTINE

The first thing to do is to get your daily schedule set. Everything will depend on when your classes are scheduled, of course, and almost every activity you do will be subject to class time.

Your first priority in school is school. Almost everything you do should be done with school in mind. But don't get me wrong; social and fun activities have their place, as long as their place is lower on your list of priorities than getting your work done.

Your daily routine does not have to be set in stone. Make it flexible enough for some of those unforeseen things that always seem to happen during a school day. For me, one of the great things about being a college student was the spontaneous events that would occur frequently; frat house parties, Greek 'walk' 'shows and march-downs, discussions on whatever square or 'set' the brothers and sisters hung out at. Being in on 'what was happening' is the major social advantage to living on campus. Every college student should spend some time during the day, if you can spare it, just hanging out and getting to know classmates.

Before you make up a daily schedule, get to know yourself and how long it may take you to establish a specific task. And for goodness sakes, BE REALISTIC! For example, it may take you anywhere from 45 minutes to two hours to prepare yourself for public consumption. If so, does it make sense to get up at 7:30 am to try to make it to an 8 am class on time?

Here was my typical Monday/Wednesday/Friday schedule during my first quarter of law school, which consisted of four class sessions three days a week, with two additional class sessions on Tuesday and Thursday:

6:45 am	out of bed
7:20 am	leave home on bike
7:45-7:50	arrive at school
8-9 am	first class
9:10-10:10 am	second class
10:10-11:25 am	break: review notes for third class
11:30-12:30 pm	third class
12:30-1:50 pm	break:review notes for fourth class
1:50-3 pm	fourth class
3-4 pm	hang out
5 pm	arrive back home
5 pm-6 pm	cook, eat, read newspaper
6-7 pm	watch news
8 pm-1 am	study with breaks as necessary
1 am	Yoga, shower, bed

As you can see, there is built-in 'flex time' in this schedule for nonessential activities between 3 pm and 7 pm every day. That four-hour period could be used in a crunch to study, do research, or whatever.

Here are some good general guidelines for managing your time wisely:

List tomorrow's activities tonight, preferably just before you go to bed. That way you don't have to rush to compile a list the next morning. Bedtime's usually quiet and you can think much more clearly than the next morning during the mad rush to get ready for class.

Do the most important things first. Prioritize the list in order of importance.

Break big jobs into smaller ones. That prevents you from being overwhelmed by the sheer size of the job you have to do.

Work on only one thing at a time; get it done and out of the way. There is nothing more frustrating than working on two or three things at the same time and never completing any of them.

Specifically define all jobs to be done. Don't write "study Econ text" on your list. Instead, you should "read and outline Chapter 12, Econ text". Again, this prevents frustration. The more specific the job, the easier it is to do and the sooner you can tell when you are finished.

Check yourself often. That way you can keep from getting caught in 'time warps': messing around in the cafeteria or watching the soaps or doing other non-productive activity.

Be realistic in making your list. Do not give yourself fifty things to do when you know you can only do five. If those other tasks can be done another day, do them another day. Otherwise you'll look at that 'monster' list, get discouraged, and be beaten before you've started. Continuously carrying over jobs from one day to the next ain't any fun, either, so be realistic.

Give yourself a reward once you've accomplished your goals for the day. A candy bar, a movie, a date: whatever it takes to congratulate yourself.

HOW TO GET THE BIGGEST BANG FOR YOUR STUDY TIME

For the ordinary student, studying is the pits. It is no fun at all. It is drudgery. A necessary evil. A means to the ultimate end, which is making a passing grade rather than learning something.

That's not a good attitude, but I firmly believe that is the general attitude of most of today's American students. However, I believe that you can have that attitude, be a successful student, and accidentally learn something if you have discipline.

The keys are (1) repetition and (2) mental submission of your mind to the material. We have already covered how the process of repetition works with speed reading; here, we will discuss repetition in the context of note-taking. But before we do that, let's focus on 'mental submission'.

Submit To The Material. Mental submission, in its simplest form, is total concentration on the task at hand. Concentration is a characteristic that all great clutch athletes have. It is the ability to block out what is going on around you; crowd noise, visual distractions, defeatist thoughts, etc., so that you get the job done. Again, though some people seem to have a natural gift of concentration, it can also be learned the usual way: by doing it.

I can't give you a magical or easy formula for learning how to concentrate on studying, but I can give you some simple help. First of all, if you are easily disturbed by noise and people, don't try to study in the student union building, cafeteria or bowling alley. If you know you have little or no willpower when it comes to saying no, don't study in a public place where you know your friends will gather and eventually ask you to hang out with them.

Experiment with different study locations and settings. Do what is best for you, rather than following arbitrary rules such as, 'always study in the library. ' If you can't study in dead silence, turn on your stereo or the radio. If you must have music, instrumental music is the most suitable because anything with vocals will get in the way of your 'mental voice' that talks in your head while you are reading.

The key question: how much mental effort will it take for you to block out distractions? Study under conditions that maximize the mind power you can use to study. If you have to spend time and effort blocking out the music, or you are on your feet dancing every five seconds, you cannot make the most efficient and effective use of your study time.

Pour yourself into what you are reading. Let it suck you in. Become absorbed in it. Don't fight against it. Concentrate on it. If somebody has to smack you upside the head to get your attention while you are studying, you are doing it the right way. It will be reflected in your grades and hopefully in your attitude about the subject you are studying, even if you hate it. Besides, you may accidentally learn something.

More hints for power-packed, big-bang studying:

Sit down and do it. The worst thing about studying is the dread that you feel before you study. The hardest step is the first one. Once you overcome that "I'd rather be doing anything else but this" feeling, you have won half the battle. Remember, motivation follows action. If you begin to study, you will feel like studying once you have studied for a while.

Take an interest in what you are studying. No matter how bad you think the subject or the teacher is, there is always something that should make you curious about a topic. Find that something and use it to increase your enthusiasm and to lessen the drudgery of studying.

Take regular breaks, but don't fidget. Use the bathroom before you start. Don't get up and look out the window every five minutes. Don't look up every time there's movement in the room. Have extra pens, pencils, paper, etc. within reach. If you have been studying diligently for a while and your mind starts to wander, take a ten-minute break. Most experts think a ten-minute break for every hour of studying is sufficient. Remember the theory of 'first-last' discussed in the previous chapter.

Study in a well-lighted area. This will keep eye strain to a minimum, decrease tiredness, and allow you to study longer. Over the years, it will possibly save your vision.

<u>Review your notes just before you go to bed</u>. That will give your mind a chance to subconsciously go over the material while you are asleep. Some folks keep pen and paper at the bedside in case of a sudden inspiration during the night. You would be surprised how this will make you more comfortable with the material you are studying.

<u>Rewrite Your Notes</u>. Repetition, as we have previously discussed, is a key factor in study efficiency and effectiveness. Some students have found it very helpful to rewrite their class notes regularly as a way of reinforcing the day's class lectures. I would highly recommend you do this daily, or at least weekly.

Rewriting notes also serves another crucial function: you can reconstruct, if necessary, the class lecture and complete or fill in anything you have missed. How many times have you tried to take notes in class only to find out two weeks later, as you study for a test, that you can't even tell if your notes were written in English or some other language? Rewriting notes avoids this trap. If you missed something you can get it from a classmate or ask the instructor to repeat or clarify the points you missed when you go back to class.

<u>Get A Tutor</u>. If you don't understand something, don't be too proud to say so. Almost all schools have a tutoring program. Some large white schools which may be holdovers to the affirmative action days of the 1970s may still have remedial programs primarily for minorities.

At the University of Florida, there were two brothers who were responsible for the continued progress and eventual graduation of many a Black grad student: Adlancy Horne and Kunle Ogundele. Both were motivated to try to help the brothers and sisters; both were geniuses in more than one field of knowledge. Just the fact that these brothers were interested enough in my academic welfare to the point of always making themselves available was very important. A friendly Black face and a word of encouragement works wonders for your academic self-esteem.

<u>Get RELIABLE Study Partners, or become part of a RELIABLE study</u>

group. I define a study partner as an individual with whom you study, day in and day out, for a particular class, subject, or major. A study group is a group of three or more students who get together only occasionally for study of a particular class or subject.

HOW TO CHOOSE A STUDY GROUP

The Bible, in Ecclesiastes 4: 9-12, says this:

Two are better than one because they have a good return for their labor. For if either of them falls, the one will lift up his companion. But woe to the one who falls when there is not another to lift him up...And if one can overpower him who is alone, two can resist him. A cord of three strands is not quickly torn apart. (New American Standard version).

I believe this passage contains good advice for students. This advice became very real in my life during my tenure in the Master of Business Administration program.

My first day of class, there were only two other Blacks in attendance; one was a brother named Kenneth C. Jacobs. He was married, had a child, and his wife Angela was in law school during part of his graduate education. He was the first and only Black student enrolled in a new joint Master of Business/Master of Health and Hospital Administration program at the University of Florida at that time. Neither one of us had business backgrounds.

We talked after class, and decided to get together to discuss ideas learned in class, exchange notes, etc.

As the next three-plus years wore on, Ken and I became close friends. We studied together, shared notes and information, took classes together when we could, became confidants in each other. Usually we would prepare for tests separately; I would prepare an outline, then we would get together and go over it, with him making corrections. After giving Ken a corrected copy of the outline, we would then split up, take sample tests, and call each other for questions or for emotional uplift.

There were many days that neither one of us thought we could make it, and spent hours either fuming or crying over test scores and grades. But academically and emotionally, we held on to each other and we both graduated with two graduate degrees. Ken was the first Black recipient of that particular joint degree.

Brothers and sisters, it CAN be done. You CAN succeed with help from other Black folks, contrary to popular myth.

Let's look closely at what the Bible passage cited above says, sentence by sentence.

1. THEY have a good return for THEIR labor. The words are plural, not singular. Therefore, in a study group, or if you have a single study partner, **EVERYBODY** must work.

So many times when you have a study group, you have freeloaders. Dead weight. Folks who feel that they can improve their test scores by association with good students like you. DO NOT get involved with somebody who will not pull his or her own weight! Successful study groups and partnerships are successful because everybody has prepared to discuss the material BEFORE the group gets together. If a member is not prepared or has not done an assignment given to him by the group, he or she should be confronted immediately and be made to understand that this is serious business, because it is.

You implicitly give up a certain amount of control of your exam preparation to another person when you join or form a study group. As the Scripture implies, the labor of the one will affect the return or reward of the whole group.

A study group should be lean and mean, as should a partnership. The larger the group, the greater the number of schedules that must be coordinated and the harder it is to get everybody together. In my experience, 3 partners (including you) is the maximum. Study groups can be larger, depending on the amount of work, the type of topic or subject, and the type of people in the group.

2. If either of them falls, the one will lift up his companion. This is the major advantage to a study partnership or group. If you are having a problem with a subject area, usually there is someone who can help. Also, if you are emotionally depressed, your study partner or

group mates can often give you that emotional lift we all sometimes need to 'get over the hump'. In fact, a primary characteristic of an effective group should be concern for the individuals within that group.

The problem, particularly with an all-Black study group at a predominantly white school, is that it can quickly become a social group rather than a study group. Brothers and sisters may use the group's discussion time to talk about the school pressures, what happened in class, what a racist dog the professor is, and so on. Because we may not have a chance to interact on a purely social level during a busy school day, when we get together we can't wait to talk to each other.

Beware of this time trap. When it's time to do business, be serious. There is plenty of time to gossip, if you must, after the meeting is over.

Some brothers and sisters have solved this problem by either forming or joining interracial groups. This serves a couple of purposes: (1) it forces the Black student to always be prepared, because none of us want to be embarrassed in front of a white person; (2) since Blacks and whites generally don't move in the same social circles, the social chatter that occurs is kept to a minimum. We'll talk more about integrated study group dynamics later.

3. <u>But woe to the one who falls when there is not another to lift him up</u>. School at times is a lonely and depressing experience. One of the main reasons why is because of the nature of the learning process.

Learning a new piece of information is something that each and every human being can only do for himself. Technology cannot transplant brains or clone people, at least not at the time that this book was written. You cannot hit another person on the head with a history book and expect all the facts in that book to be transferred to that person's mind.

Therefore, in a sense, education is one of the most solitary pursuits known to man. Anybody can attempt to teach you something, but nobody can learn anything for you. Think about <u>that</u> for a minute.

Despite the alone-ness of education, interacting with others who are sharing the same educational experiences can be invaluable to you. Study partners and groups can serve this vital function.

4. <u>And if one can overpower him who is alone, two can resist him.</u>

Make no mistake about it: we are all in a battle against the negative forces of this world. A lot of students are losing this battle by falling prey to depression, lack of self-confidence, isolation, self-consciousness and paranoia, among other things. That is why we see sudden rashes of high school and college suicides and rampant drug abuse even at the elementary school levels. So many students think that no one understands or is willing to help.

Not true. Without getting preachy, God knows and understands. I personally believe informed, fervent, sincere and effectual prayer changes things.

Secondly, your classmates and teachers can identify with your struggle. You are not totally alone; seek help from others around you, including those in your study group, or professional psychological counseling, if necessary.

5. A cord of three strands is not quickly torn apart. I believe this passage to mean that two people held together by God are not easily torn apart, much like a rope made of three cords is more secure than a rope made only of two cords. Though this principle is usually applied to marriage, it also can be applied to any close human relationship.

My friend Ken and I never discussed whether God was a part of us going through a rigorous academic program together. In retrospect, I believe He was, and I thank Him for placing us in that situation so that we could be so helpful to each other.

HOW TO CHOOSE AN INSTRUCTOR AND REGISTER FOR CLASSES

Usually all colleges have more than one instructor teaching a subject. If that is the case, how do you do choose which instructor to take? What do you look for? There are a number of important considerations: your self-assessment, the instructor's teaching style, and the instructor's grading system.

If possible, meet the instructor personally before you sign up for class. Ask her whether the class is lecture or Socratic, how she grades (does she 'curve' grades? This is good to know in a class that will be especially tough for all the students). Ask for a copy of the exam schedule if the instructor has one. Ask about test types: true-false, multichoice, short answer, essay.

Get the 'scoop' from other students who have taken her class. What's the word on her? Is she fair? Does she know what she is talking about? Is she accessible and receptive to students? Does she rework old exams, or change them from semester to semester?

Use your self-assessment of your strengths and weaknesses to determine whether you will probably do well in the class. If you hate numbers and have always had a hard time even in basic math courses, does it make sense to take an advanced math class which consists of nothing but working math problems? Try to match your strengths and weaknesses with the teaching method the instructor will use.

Here is a simple chart to help guide your decisions.

IF YOU...	THINK ABOUT TAKING...
are a morning person	early morning classes
are a night owl	late classes and classes that begin in the afternoon so you can study through the night
are a good writer	classes with written assignments instead of tests and a paper instead of a final
are a number cruncher	hard numbers classes or classes that call for highly analytic thinking
have a great memory	classes with periodic objective exams
are practical or 'learn by doing'	lab courses, internships, classes with hands-on projects

are creative or disciplined	independent study, classes requiring creative projects, correspondence courses
are verbally quick and outgoing	small seminar classes, classes taught by Socratic method, or where extra credit is given for class participation
learn best from hearing	lecture classes
learn best from reading	classes with heavy reading assignments

If you had an instructor that has 'done you justice', find out what other classes she is teaching and take them again. Grab hold and don't let go! Ride that horse to death. The advantages: she will remember your beautiful face from previous classes; you know her grading system; she knows from experience you are a motivated student, thus is more willing to give you the benefit of the doubt in grading you; she can become a mentor that will come to your rescue in the crunch.

IMAGE MANAGEMENT: PRACTICAL WAYS TO MANIPULATE INSTRUCTORS AND ADMINISTRATORS

You have chosen the instructors; you've gone through the whole registration hassle; you've set up your schedules; you've learned the memory and note-taking systems. It's the first day of class.

Time to work on THEM.

Why should you be concerned about your image? Because the perception of you as a student can have a definite effect on your GPA, especially when you are on the line for a C+ or B, a pass or fail. Your perception to an administrator can also affect whether you graduate on time or even at all. Instructors and administrators are subject to the same whims, likes and dislikes as anybody else.

I can't impress upon you enough how important it is to control the image the instructor has of you. After all, if you attend a predominately white school, you stick out like a sore thumb anyway because of the color of your skin. You may as well put the best foot forward. If you are at a predominantly Black school, you still must concern yourself with your image for all the other reasons listed in this chapter.

Image management assumes one fact: the overwhelming majority of instructors, no matter what they say, will give the benefit of the doubt to a student who is aggressively attempting to learn the material. Simply said, teachers will reward you for effort.

Image management is a tactic which makes the instructor think you are breaking your neck to learn his or her materials, which ain't necessarily so. But as you'll see, it's not necessarily easy.

Before we go on, let me say this: The following information in this section is <u>NOT</u> to be used alone! It is to be used <u>ONLY</u> in conjunction with the rest of the strategies outlined in this book. Though any instructor or administrator can be fooled temporarily, if you don't have some substance behind the image you have built, you are dead meat come grade time.

Here are some ways to make a teacher think you are a study animal:

<u>Make an appointment with your instructor in the first two-three weeks of the semester or before the first test</u>. You can use this visit to feel him out, as well as plant the seed. If you have not been given a class schedule or syllabus, ask about grade policies, test dates, etc. Also, ask about supplementary reading or suggested outside sources. Some instructors take outlines and examples directly from a related textbook.

If you need a certain grade out of this class, let the instructor know NOW! For example if you are a senior who needs an A to graduate, you would be foolish to wait until after you had flunked the first two tests to tell the instructor.

If you are in this kind of situation, let the instructor know that you are willing to do anything (within the boundaries of the law and your own morality), including extra assignments, papers, study sessions, independent study, etc. to get the grade you need.

Be a good consumer. Ask about office hours. Ask if he is available for study sessions before the exams with interested class members. Ask whether you can call after hours at home if you are stuck on a problem. This is a fairly common practice in graduate programs. If you think it is appropriate, ask for his or her home phone, and the hours you may call. Be careful with this, especially if you are a woman; many instructors, especially men, are extremely leery of possible sexual harassment charges.

<u>Go to the instructor as soon as possible with questions</u>. Many times fellow students or study group mates can explain confusing concepts to your satisfaction. If you still have a problem, go to the instructor as soon as possible for help.

I personally think it's distasteful and demeaning to stand around the instructor immediately after class to ask a question, like so many others seem to do. Many students use this as an opportunity to do a little 'brown-nosing.' How disgusting. You can do these same thing, be less obvious about it, and probably get a less hurried, more understandable answer to your questions.

Unless you have a burning question that you absolutely must have answered that minute, it is better tactically and a more efficient use of your time to go the instructor's office. There you have more time in a less frantic atmosphere, compared to asking a question in the midst of the chaos of a class lecture that has just ended.

If you really want to get fancy before you meet the instructor in his office, do some research on him. If he is a Ph.D., there is a book called <u>Dissertation Abstracts</u> that will give you a short summary of what his dissertation was all about. It will give you an idea of what his academic interests are.

A visit to the office also gives you an idea of the type of person he is, since most offices are reflective of the occupant's personality. For instance, if you see pictures of Buckwheat, a mounted Rebel flag, and a picture of Martin Luther King, Jr. on his dart board, you may want to consider dropping the class.

<u>Before you ask questions of an instructor, do your homework!</u> Of all

the image management hints in this book, this is the most important. Absolutely nothing will shoot you down in flames quicker than asking a question that shows you haven't read the assigned materials.

This is true whether you are asking a question in class or in the office. Be sure you have read all of the assignments. Think about what you want to ask before you open your mouth. If you are in class, listen to your classmates' questions. If somebody asks a question either identical or substantially similar to yours, don't ask your question.

Observe proper classroom etiquette. Try to get to class on time. (This was my biggest problem.) If you are late, don't come in 'skinning and grinning', talking loud. Sit down as soon and as discreetly as possible. Raise your hand whenever you want to be recognized; don't scream out questions or answers.

Try to sit in the front of the class, if possible, so that you can see and hear clearly. This is especially important with foreign instructors with heavy accents, or soft-spoken instructors. Also, eye contact is very important. It lets the instructor know that you are interested in what he has to say, even if you are not.

If you do have some feeling or reaction to what the instructor is saying, then let your face show it. Most instructors prefer some emotion, even negative, rather than a blank face.

If you are called upon unexpectedly and you don't know the answer, don't fake it. Don't try to improvise. Admit it and sit down, rather than waste the class' time.

If you make an appointment or drop by and the instructor is not in, leave a note. Simple, but effective. It can say something like this:

12/31/87 Doctor Feelgood: Came by to see you about homework problem. Charles Cherry, Economics 101, 12:30 pm

When the instructor returns, there is a written record of your visit. The seed that you are willing to go the extra mile has again been planted.

If you make an appointment and have to miss it, let the instructor know in advance. If you can't contact him by phone, leave a note early in the day with the time on it. If the cancellation is very late, call the department office, his secretary, or home and leave a message with somebody.

Complete your assignments on time. If you can't, give a good reason why you didn't. If you had a death in the family, show him the funeral program. If you were deathly ill, show him the doctor's note or hospital bracelet. It's best to alleviate any doubt up front rather than having the instructor question your integrity.

Meet with your instructor periodically whether you have grade problems or not, but especially if you have grade problems. When you get a test paper back, go over it individually with the instructor if possible. Ask him specifically what he was looking for in the answers to the questions, especially in essay questions. Ask him to give you a written model essay answer. This will give you an idea of how he thinks and grades; it will pay huge dividends on the next exam. It also again reinforces the instructor's perception that you are willing to work for your grade.

If you are having a problem with a particular concept, ask the instructor to give you a problem to work out to test your understanding of the concept. Have him take a look at it.

Teachers hate students who are invisible during most of the term, but who come to their office steaming and carping about grades and tests. They also hate students who try to emotionally manipulate them via personal, brown-nosing, buddy-buddy type relationships just for a grade.

Don't be afraid to compliment the instructor if the compliment is sincere. Most of them aren't teaching for the money.

These are only a few of the image management tactics you can use. Use your own imagination; work within your own 'zone of comfort'. If you are morally comfortable with 'image management' techniques, anything you can do that increases the instructor's belief in the perception that you are a serious student should be done.

As you can see, all of these tactics demand work, prior preparation, desire and motivation. You may be doing some of these already. If so, keep it up and refine your techniques.

IMAGE MANAGEMENT AND ADMINISTRATORS

A few ground rules you should know about dealing with the institutional administration:

<u>School, especially at the administrative level, is a cold-blooded business and should be treated as such.</u> Colleges are business organizations. They are in the business of education, and you are a consumer. In America, consumers have rights. Because you are a student doesn't mean you are a slave.

The whole academic environment, the physical plant, the academic titles, the pomp and circumstance at graduation, all serve the same purpose as do elevated benches and judge's robes in the court system: to mystify the public. All that stuff is designed to intimidate the average person and create a sense of awe and obedience to the wishes of the people in charge.

<u>Administrators and instructors are not God.</u> Administrators have power, but you have legal rights that you can assert if need be. Specifically, they are highly susceptible to complaints of racial and sexual discrimination, though not as much as in the recent past. If you want to see some fur fly, go into any major state university president's office and scream, "RACIAL DISCRIMINATION!" at the top of your lungs and leave a lawyer's business card.

<u>Education is a system. You must decide whether to operate within it, given your personality, principles, and goals.</u> Students come and go, but the institution is perpetual. And according to the statistics, Black students seem to go earlier (via flunking out) or stay later (via slow academic progress) than anybody else.

Keep your place within the institution in perspective. If you keeled over and died in the registration line, folks would just step over your body as the line moved forward. Institutional life would go on.

Remember this when you are trying to change a grade, get financial aid, or whatever. Trying to foster a massive change in the educational system is like trying to chip away a glacier with a blunt toothpick. The more you know about the nature of how the system works, the more you can maneuver within it, and possibly manipulate it, for your benefit.

I am not saying you should let the administration run over you, or continue its involvement in odious and unethical activities. Black students have usually been intimately involved with student protest movements of all kinds.

But for goodness sakes, don't flunk out or lose your financial aid while you are carrying a picket sign, while your genius friends picketing with you are being funded from their trust fund left to them by a rich uncle or something.

Remember also that the people who run the institution are people. If you get upset at one of the clerks and act a public fool, what good will it do? Which brings us to the next point.

When you have a real problem, keep going up the ladder of authority until you get to someone with the authority to make a decision, or go immediately to the person who made the mistake. Don't mess around too long with the 'hired help' who won't be able to solve your problem. Follow the chain of command. DOCUMENT in writing who you talked to, what was said, and when it was said. Another hint: If you get into a dispute with the hired help, DON'T discuss the problem with the administrator in the presence of the workers if at all possible. It may force a weak administrator to back the worker to prevent a mutiny. Still you must...

Treat the 'hired help' with human respect and decency. I am not using the term 'hired help' here in an arrogant fashion, because the truth is that the administrators are really the peons. Most of the career employees who work in 'lower' positions and for less pay know the system backwards and forwards, because many have worked in their positions for years. If you get them angry, they can send you halfway around the world and you will end up with nothing. If you treat them like human beings, they can cut a lot of red tape for you. Never think that you are too good, too 'educated' to talk to them and ask questions.

The school catalog is the administrators' bible. Learn how to use it for your best interests. Remember the fat little book the school sent you when you applied for admission? The one with the nice picture of the school on the cover? Well, that book that you probably threw away is one of the most important books you'll ever receive in your college career.

It's called the school catalog. In it are the administrative rules and regulations, the sequences and descriptions of courses and majors, financial aid information, and all kinds of other juicy stuff.

Knowledge of the catalog can make or break you should you become caught in an administrative squeeze somewhere along the way. You should at least have a general working knowledge of it. And whenever you have to go to an administrator about some problem consult the catalog first. If it helps your case, cite chapter and verse to the administrator.

If possible, NEVER put yourself in a position where an administrator must 'use her discretion' unless you are absolutely sure that the ruling will be in your favor. Otherwise the administrator has the opportunity to screw you within the rules.

For example, the catalog says you can drop a class within 10 days of signing up for it without losing the money you put out for it. After 10 days, it's at the discretion of the department chairperson. If at all possible, drop the class within the 10 days.

Get the administrator's decision on your case in writing. This is crucial when a decision is made that may be different from standard operating procedure. Don't be embarrassed to do this! Administrators drop dead; or they take new jobs and move away. Why should you suffer because of that?

The best way to do this is to write a little note with your request and ask him to sign it. If he is reluctant, tell him it's to prevent the bureaucrats who keep up with such things from calling his office for verification. After he signs, immediately photocopy for your files.

Fill out all necessary forms properly and promptly and copy them for your files. Copying and filing everything will save you untold amounts of grief, especially when some school bureaucrat says they "never received" this form or that or lost it somehow.

And please don't do something stupid like forge an instructor's name on a form. It's not right and you may get caught.

Get into the information flow. This is so important! Unlike high school, college administrators don't go out of their way to tell you anything. There are no loudspeaker announcements before morning classes. Get into the habit of reading the school newspaper whenever it comes out and checking bulletin boards, ESPECIALLY financial aid.

Administrators and instructors do and will communicate with each other about you. If you are in a jam, the administrators will get your transcripts and probably contact one of your instructors about you. If your image is one of an aggressive, interested, hard-working student, you will probably come out on top, even if your grades aren't the best in the world.

But if none of your previous instructors know you or one puts the 'bad mouth' on you, you can probably hang it up. THAT'S when all the time and effort of image management becomes worthwhile.

PIGEONHOLING THE PROFESSORS

Ready for a profound statement?

Every Person Is An Individual. Very deep, right?

But though every person is different from every other, sometimes folks can be generally classified, or 'pigeonholed,' by how they perform their jobs. Instructors and administrators are no different.

Here are some instructors (and one administrator) I have met during my academic career. Their qualities are only slightly exaggerated.

Dean X: He or she is Dean in charge of minority affairs, or some such title. The 'X' is because the Dean's real name changes every year due to high turnover.

From the administration's standpoint, Dean X's job is to keep the natives from getting too restless by distributing welfare checks (oops, I mean financial aid) on time and by making sure that the supply of Black bodies in the school doesn't decrease. Dean X also runs the school's student affirmative action program, as long as he doesn't get too affirmative.

God help Dean X if he or she begins to take the job too seriously by pushing hard for Black students, by demanding more money for recruitment, by getting more funding sources, or by increasing the numbers of Black students who actually graduate! All of a sudden Dean X is given "additional responsibilities" that will take up time from focusing on minority affairs. Or, Dean X may get battle fatigue and decide to give it all up. Dean X has found out what other Dean X's already know: the job is dead-end. If you push too hard, you're gone;

if you don't keep the bodies enrolled (not striving toward a degree, but just enrolled), you're gone.

Go visit Dean X whenever you can. He or she would appreciate a good word from a Black student every now and then. Most of them are sincerely concerned about the educational well-being of Black students.

Dr. Dashiki, also known as Professor Rambro: This is the resident Black radical on campus. He was probably hired during the late 60s and early 70s, when Affirmative Action was extended to the faculty as the "right thing to do".

Dr. Dashiki is his own personal fashion statement. He still wears his dashiki (hence his name), leather sandals, steel-rimmed glasses a la Malcolm X, and jeans. During the winter he is absolutely breathtaking, fashionably attired in a red, black and green knit skullcap and kente scarf.

But don't let the sharp dress fool you. The man has a mind like a steel trap and the fearlessness of a commando (hence the name Professor Rambro). Malcolm, Martin, Marcus Garvey, Frederick Douglass, Paul Robeson; all were mere boys compared to this giant of a man. He searches out opportunities to pull the tiger's tail, i.e. attack the administration on behalf of an issue or student. He'll do it for you, as long as you fit into his political agenda. After all, he's tenured, so what is he worried about? It's only your academic career that may be twisting in the wind.

What a guy.

Dr. Darkmeat: He is just the opposite of Professor Rambro. Black, but a true chicken.

Probably hired in the late '70s or early '80s, this instructor, male or female (most likely male), wouldn't take a stand if his life depended on it. He is scared of his own shadow. He would never help any student, Black or white, because he would be afraid of the repercussions from the administration. Therefore, he is an equal opportunity coward.

Our misdirection strategy is the only method of dealing with this shell of a man because it gives him justifiable reasons for cutting you a break and defending himself before the administration, which is his worst nightmare.

He is pitiful. The major reason why is because he is afraid to get too close to Black students, since he doesn't want to have a reputation of 'favoring' Blacks. Meanwhile, his white counterparts are giving grades away to hot cheerleaders, students who are their drinking partners, etc.

Dr. Darkmeat has a friend who teaches at the school. They are probably distant relatives. His name is...

Professor Oreo: He is a bigger threat to you than Dr. Darkmeat. Darkmeat will stiff-arm you and try to give you some distance. Oreo will welcome you like a brother, then screw you.

The most insidious way that Oreo works is that he will actually grade you <u>tougher</u> than many white instructors will in order to prove to everybody that he plays no favorites. Meanwhile, he's on this minority commission, advisor for that Black organization, and is cited as a role model for students. But when you talk to this brother (or sister) personally, you find out that he or she has <u>no</u> Black consciousness whatsoever; no appreciation of our history, no concern for the future of our people.

The Earth Mother/Godfather of Soul: Thank God for these two. There seems to be one or two in every major university, one of the few Black faculty or administrators who feel personally responsible for the success of Black students.

The Earth Mother reminds you so much of your own mother, grandmother or favorite aunt it's uncanny. She is your bridge over troubled academic waters. She gives you a pat on the head when you need it; she gives you a tongue-lashing when you deserve it. She has probably been a professor for a while and has resisted the temptation of becoming the next Dean X so that she can stay in the classroom. She is enthusiastic about her profession and is willing to go to bat for Black students collectively and individually. Sometimes she is used, abused, and disappointed by Black students but she still comes back for more. Above everything else, she loves to see Black students give school everything they have. But if you really want to alienate her, lie to her.

The Godfather of Soul is the Earth Mother's male counterpart. When he talks, people listen. If you can take a class from either one of them, do so. It will do your self-esteem a world of good.

The Godfather of Ego: In contrast to the Godfather of Soul, this

Godfather gets a kick out of being placed on a pedestal by Black students. Sometimes the word will get out, "if you're in academic trouble, the Godfather of Ego can get you out." That may be true, but you've got to play by the Godfather's rule. His primary rule is "stroke my ego. Lick my toes."

My brother or sister, you are on your own in dealing with this egomaniac. Just remember our discussion on principle vs. ego in Chapter 2.

<u>Dr. Demented</u>: Along with the Earth Mother and the Godfather of Soul this is my favorite category.

Most of the time he is considered nutty by the other professors. That's because Dr. Demented uses imagination in class. He doesn't always teach from books. He forces students to use their common sense.

I remember two professors very fondly. One was an economics instructor who once took off his pants and underwear in class and cut the waistband out of his BVD's to illustrate the economic concept of 'elasticity'.

Another professor I enjoyed greatly was a law professor, a native of Germany who spoke English with a pronounced German accent. He's white, about 6 feet 4 inches tall, 220 pounds, bald and very pale. He would go into some of the roughest Black bars and lounges in town, take a seat, strike up a conversation with the brothers, watch people, and come back to class to tell us what impact economic status has on interviewing a potential legal client. I know some <u>Black</u> folks who wouldn't even speak to a person who frequents the kinds of places this man has visited.

These guys were different. Grades were unimportant to them. They wanted to force students to think. You remembered what they taught you and you could apply it. That's the name of the game.

<u>Professor Shakespeare</u>: To him, the classroom is a stage and every day a chance for a different performance. He is great at presenting the material in an entertaining and informative manner.

The problem is, he can't improvise. He follows his teaching plan so carefully that he gets upset if you ask a question that causes him to think. His major concern is not teaching you the material, but presenting it to you at all costs.

If you run into one of these, the best thing to do is not to ask too many questions in class, and to be sure and take good notes. Any questions that you have should be addressed to him one-on-one.

Dr. Jack Nicholson/Glenn Close: Imagine Jack Nicholson (who starred as the Joker in the "Batman" movie) or Glenn Close (who was the mentally deranged mistress in the movie "Fatal Attraction") teaching a class full of students and you've got an accurate picture of this instructor.

He or she is vicious. You risk your life asking a question because he will cut you up in small pieces with his tongue. He believes so strongly in what he is teaching that anyone who disagrees with it risks instant death from those death-ray eyes.

Lots of ego stroking needed here, and only in the instructor's office. Never confront this type in the classroom, if possible. You'll pay for it later, somewhere down the line, if you do.

Professor Harrylegs: A female instructor, and a liberated one at that. Refuses to shave her legs; no slave to fashion and conventional hygiene, this one. Usually extremely competent, she and Dr. Dashiki are on the same wavelength. A great ally to have, but also with the same limitations as Dr. Dashiki.

Dr. Halashabamala: Usually a resident alien, a graduate exchange student, or a recent U.S. citizen. Occasionally brilliant, sometimes he speaks with a heavy accent which makes his English almost incomprehensible. Seems to be concentrated in hard science fields and at the business schools and drives the students there crazy. Knowing this, the administration has him teaching five classes a day, the largest number of students in the department. Sheer torture.

Instructor Joe Cool: One of the all-time jerks, along with Dr. Oreo. Joe Cool just wants to be loved. He wants to be one of the boys. So when students begin to complain about the pace of the class, old Joe begins to go slower. What he doesn't tell you is that you will still be responsible for stuff that he doesn't cover in class.

Joe also seems to be very pro-student. He, like the Oreo, is a high-profile advisor and he plays the I-love-even-students-and-roaches game well.

What I hate about the Joe Cool types is hobnobbing with them may have an effect on your grade, even if you never show effort or even come to class. Therefore, our manipulation strategy may be of limited use here. Advice: watch him, stay up on the materials, and be prepared to do some serious scrambling to prepare yourself for the exams.

ADD/DROP, AND MANIPULATING THE SYSTEM TO YOUR BENEFIT

Occasionally, you'll find yourself having to add or drop a class, for various reasons. Maybe you have a conflict with a required class. Maybe you've just found out your favorite instructor is back in the saddle this semester.

Consider registering for one class more than you will actually take. For instance, if you want to take five classes for the semester, register for six and attend all six up until the end of the add-drop grace period, which is usually two weeks or so. Then you can drop the class you don't want and not have to pay fees for it. This little trick allows you to reserve a spot in a class that may fill up quickly. Bear in mind, however, that you may hurt some other students who need to take the course you registered for, but dropped. They may have had to take an alternate course, because you took their spot.

ADDING A CLASS:

Go directly to the instructor. If the class is full, tell him so, and give good reasons why you want to take the class. Since the instructors are usually the ones who set the maximum numbers for their classes, they can make exceptions. Let the instructor know that you are willing to sit in on the class until some lazy stiff (I mean, student) has to drop it before the end of the add-drop period.

If you know you want to register for a class that requires a prerequisite that you have not taken, check the catalog to see if that situation is covered. If the catalog is silent about taking a class without the prerequisite, the instructor may have discretion to waive it. See him before registration and inform him of the situation.

If you must add a class after add-drop, be prepared to hustle because you are going to be at least two weeks behind.

Also you should know that it is much easier to add a class than to drop one. Go to the instructor and let him know you want to add his class and that you want to catch up as quickly as possible. Use the opportunity to let him know that you are the <u>exception to the rule.</u> He may refer you to the chairman of the department; but if the instructor says OK, usually the administration will go along.

DROPPING A CLASS:

There are valid reasons for dropping a class. The most valid is because you are flunking it. But we know that's not gonna happen, right?

Let's examine other reasons for and consequences of dropping classes.

<u>You are not academically prepared for the class.</u> There are only three ways this excuse is acceptable to me. First, that you are freshman who mistakenly registered for a Ph.D. course. Second, you have not taken a prerequisite that is crucial to understanding the course. Third, some major catastrophe has happened in your life: death, serious illness, etc. There are no other acceptable excuses for not being prepared for class after you have been there more than two weeks.

<u>You have a serious personality conflict with the professor.</u> Possibly valid, depending on the circumstances. You aren't gonna love all your professors, but you should be able to tolerate all of them, even the Dr. Oreos and the Joe Cool types. But if you believe that the instructor is really going to mess with your grade; if the course is crucial to you for some reason; or if it's in your major, you should seriously consider bailing out.

The consequences of dropping a class depend upon when you drop it, and what is in the school catalog. If it's dropped during the add-drop period, the school usually won't charge you for the class and the class won't appear on your transcript. If you drop it after add-drop, the school will probably make you pay for the hours. Also, most schools will give you either a WP (withdrew with a passing grade) or a WF (withdrew with a failing grade) on your transcript.

One thing you don't want to do is have WF's and WP's all over your transcript. Your first employer, who will probably be the only one who looks at your transcript, will think that you are a quitter. Besides, there are other options...

PASS-FAIL, AUDITS, 'GET OVERS,' INCOMPLETES

Exposure to these little gems of knowledge could save you in a pinch, rescue you from academic probation, or get your GPA to the Honor Roll level.

P-F (PASS-FAIL): Most schools will allow you to take a limited number of courses in which you will not receive a letter or number grade. You will only receive a Pass or a Fail grade. Usually P-Fs are not averaged into your GPA. Therefore, it makes sense to take the pass-fail option in a few situations: (a) when it's midterm and you won't get the A or B that you need, but you will pass but you don't want to drop the class; (b) when you are taking an elective, but you don't want it to affect your GPA if you don't do well; (c) when your semester load is very heavy,you don't have an easy class, and you need some more 'flex time' to study for other classes.

You should not go pass-fail when: (a) you could flunk the class (b) it's a crucial class in your major; (c) you will probably make an A in the class (d) you are thinking about transferring to another school (the other school probably won't accept the pass-fail courses).

AUDITING A CLASS: This is the term for sitting in on a class, doing the same work as your classmates and paying for it, but not receiving the credit. At first blush, it sounds crazy.

But it may be your salvation if you are having extreme difficulty passing a class that is required in your major and is a prerequisite for many other courses. Auditing gives you the opportunity to stick your hand in the fire and not get burned. If you diligently audit a class, you'll be ready to take the next semester for credit.

'GET OVERS': Also known as 'sop' or 'gut' courses. A valid, time-honored way of padding your GPA or taking it easy for the semester. The students generally know which classes and which instructors are get overs, so the classes fill up quickly. Look for things like Basic Home Economics, Arts and Crafts, Basic Human Sexuality, Relationship Between the Sexes, etc.

INCOMPLETES: An 'I' for 'Incomplete' is given to a student who has not fulfilled enough requirements to receive a grade. For example, if you miss the final for some reason, the instructor may choose to give you an 'I' instead of averaging a zero into your class grade. Note that the instructors have total discretion in when and under what circumstances to give 'I's instead of other grades.

'I's can also be life savers. Suppose you have been working with a professor all semester. He knows you have done everything possible to learn the material. You've worked the misdirection strategy to perfection. You still blow the final. You may be able to talk him into giving you an 'I' for the course and allowing you to do a paper, a project, a take-home test, or whatever, during the next semester. It won't get you an 'A', but it may get you that C that you need to stay in school.

You'd better be a student of your word, though. If you don't complete the assignment he gives you before the end of the next grading period, the 'I' automatically turns into an F. You'll also have a betrayed, upset instructor on your hands.

The usefulness of each of these options (except the Get Over) will depend, as always, on what the catalog says. You should consult it before you decide which option to exercise.

HOW TO GET A GRADE CHANGED

Like everything else, there's a way to do it and a way not to do it.

DON'T go off on the instructor in the hallway.

DO check your test or test papers immediately for numerical errors. Average your grades yourself and see what you come up with. Check all your tests to see whether you wrote your name on the top. (If not, the instructor may have recorded a zero). See if the registrar made a mistake.

THEN take the proof to the instructor. If you feel you were not given proper credit on essay questions, come prepared to argue your point. Don't lie; be straight. Don't scream and don't overstate your case.

If the poor grade was your fault, tell the instructor why. Before you speak to him about the grade, you may want to re-examine the section above on auditing and receiving an 'I'.

NOTE: At all times, be prepared to hear the word NO to your requests. Don't let this temporary obstacle defeat you.

INTERACTIONS WITH PEERS (BUSINESS/SOCIAL)

School, especially college, is a place where lifelong relationships are formed. Your school reputation will follow you for the rest of your life. If you have a reputation as a cheater, a liar, or being untrustworthy, lazy or undependable, that reputation will follow you.

The reason why this is true is because the school experience becomes the only opportunity for people who pass through your life to judge what kind of person you are. Sometimes the judgment is true; sometimes it's not.

Think about this in your own experience. For example, suppose you heard that one of your classmates was arrested for a violent crime. If you know this person only as a classmate, your mind will go to his class performance or demeanor. Based only on those limited contacts in class, you will make a snap judgment, maybe on the probability of this person's guilt or innocence.

The same thing happens 10, 20, or 30 years later. There are some folks that I went to school with that I would think twice about having a business relationship with, because they were thieving slimeballs in college. If I couldn't trust them then, how can I be sure that I can trust them now?

Your interaction with peers can be divided into types I'll call business and social.

BUSINESS interactions can be defined as relationships which focus on school (i.e. study groups, group projects, professional or academic fraternities or clubs, etc.). It is here that the most important images of you are formed. Can you pull your own weight? Are you honest? Intelligent?

We will define SOCIAL interactions as relationships with your peers that have a focus other than school (e.g. sports teams, social fraternities, etc.) They are an integral and important part of your school experience, and they should be cultivated. Note that perceptions of you can be formed through both types of interactions.

Typically Black students in white schools have problems in business relationships, especially when integrated groups are involved. To many of us, the worst assignments were group projects in which the group members were picked (supposedly) at random. Usually the Black students were split up among different groups.

You can almost depend on getting frozen out of these types of groups. Sometimes they will have meetings and not contact you. Sometimes they will ignore what you have to say. They may assign you a menial task such as making sure all group members have a copy of the final report. Basically many Black students get the feeling that this kind of group thinks that Black students have nothing to contribute.

Different Black students have different coping strategies as far as group projects are concerned. Many raise hell immediately about whatever unfair treatment they believe they have received. They believe the group members should be set straight right off the bat. Others take the opposite approach and feel that they don't have to prove anything to anybody. They lay back and wait until something happens and then raise hell. Still others do nothing at all and go with the flow, grinning and bearing it. You should pick the approach that best suits your personality.

Different Black students also have different ways of dealing with business and social interactions. Let's list some of them.

1. Low profile: This brother or sister chooses not to join organizations or draw too much attention to himself or herself. They cultivate very few business or personal relationships. These types of folks keep their mouths shut and just do their work. They may have been in class with you for four years and you may have never noticed them. They believe if they keep their heads down they won't become targets for teachers and administrators, and that they will get through, get out of school unnoticed and go on to bigger and better things.

2. High profile: These folks think that by putting themselves in the

public eye, they insulate themselves from harm by becoming too big to bring down. In short, shooting at a high profile person is like shooting at an elephant. Unless you shoot straight and with high power, the elephant won't fall. Usually these types join political organizations like fraternities, sororities, student government, etc. to get an inside track with teachers or administrators.

If you are considering this strategy, you must have a strong and fairly combative personality and lots of self-confidence.

3. White only: Some brothers and sisters in white schools choose to have both social and business relationships only with white students and teachers. They feel that only through the white students can they get total access to fraternity test files and other information that Black students know nothing about. They believe that this strategy can bring them in contact with the top students and help develop social relationships with white instructors who will remember them at grade time. Many times they do not want to associate with other Black students because their strategy is to differentiate themselves from the average Black student in the minds of the teacher or administrator.

To successfully implement this strategy, you must be totally comfortable around whites. You must be familiar with their social mores. You must also be willing to turn your back on your fellow Black students. Then you must have a strong personality and a resilient nature so that you can bounce back once this strategy blows up in your face. Because it will. Eventually.

4. Black only: Here, the Black student chooses to socialize or do business with Blacks only. No integrated study groups; no social interaction with whites, unless absolutely necessary. Pro: You can hang out with people with whom you are probably most comfortable. Cons: instructors and fellow students will probably pigeonhole you as anti-social and a Black radical-type. You won't have the opportunity to keep your 'cocktail-party' mingling skills, i.e. how to operate in the white man's world, too sharp. Also, all-Black groups sometimes develop a paranoid, permanent victim-type mentality and begin to focus on discrimination, both actual and perceived, rather than academics.

5. Black/white: Black students who take this route try to have the best of both worlds. They know that America is 'the white man's country', and they feel that they should make the best of the situation. In

fact, many brothers and sisters attend white schools to nurture and hone their social interaction skills among whites.

I believe this and strategy 4 are the predominant strategies used by Black students at white schools. The reasons are fairly simple.

Most Black students know that they must deal with whites at some point, even if they don't want to, because of the numbers involved. Black students usually don't constitute more than ten percent of the student population at any predominantly white school. The percentage of Black instructors is even smaller.

These are only a few of the particular strategies I saw used by Black students, or used myself. Note that 1 and 2 can be used in combination with 3, 4, and 5. Here is an example.

A brother that I knew in graduate school used a combination high profile-Black/white strategy to graduate from graduate school. He became active in the school's NAACP student chapter. He also was active in the Black student organizations, both undergraduate and graduate, and aligned himself with various liberal faculty organizations (environmentalists, legal aid groups, etc.) Thus, this brother was able to cloak himself in a highly potent form of political protection.

Later in the school year, there was some discrepancy in the brother's GPA to the point where it was possible that he may not graduate. The 'race problem' and the brother's political beliefs became media issues which embarrassed the school; he called in the political heavyweights in the faculty; and the rest, as they say, is history. He got his degree on time.

CULTURE SHOCK AND MISPLACED PRIORITIES

Misplaced priorities can kill a student. The biggest misplaced priority is that of social relationships, specifically recreational activities.

I am a proud graduate of Morehouse College (Morehouse men call Harvard University 'the Morehouse of the North') and the University of Florida, also known nationally as 'Suntan U.' Both are excellent schools, but the contrast could not be more striking.

Morehouse was small (less than 2000 students), all-male, all Black, located in a predominately Black metropolis, Atlanta. UF was large (more than 35,000 students), coed, mostly white, located in a small but lovely college town, Gainesville, Fla.

After touring the campus during my first week in Gainesville, I was in shock.

Bowling alleys, lighted racquetball courts, lighted tennis courts, a golf course, swimming pools between dorms, a private lake for students, big-screen TV, a full-service cafeteria; on-campus automatic bank teller machines, a video arcade, computerized registration, on-campus bus shuttle service from the parking lots, an on-campus bar and grill, private phones in dorm rooms, weight rooms, gyms for non-athletes, bike trails, a serious intramural sports program, frat houses that looked like mansions, Coke machines everywhere, parties every weekend.

Contrast my four years at Morehouse. A two-lane bowling alley under the gym that never worked. A pool for the students that was opened maybe once a week. Sauerkraut and cornbread for dinner, on occasion. A registration system that had not changed in 40 years. A frat house in which only two of six showers ever worked the two years I lived there.

Later, I learned that the academic mortality rate for Black undergrads over a four-year period was 90 percent. That meant that of 100 Black UF freshmen who enter during the same semester, only 10 would graduate in four years. I began to ask myself why.

Probably a number of the usual reasons: poor study habits, lack of discipline, etc. But another reason really stood out: culture shock.

That was what hit me right between the eyes from my first day in Gainesville, and I was already a college graduate. The more I thought about it, the more plausible it seemed. It happened to me, an honors graduate of one of America's best colleges, Black or white; a child of the emerging Black middle class. Can you imagine what it was like for those young, more impressionable brothers and sisters, new high school graduates, who may have been raised in the ghetto, or who may be the first of their families to be high school graduates?

As I looked around, my suspicions seemed to be confirmed. You could always find brothers on the 'set', playing in the intramural games, or at the Black frat/sorority parties, in the cafeteria, on the racquetball courts. You found very few at the library or at the computer lab. The whole four-plus years I was at UF I rarely saw a Black student in a library carrel at the main library. (A <u>carrel</u> is a one-person desk with 'blinders' on three sides. When you sit at one, you can't see anything or anyone else around you.)

Maybe the brothers and sisters don't like carrels; maybe they didn't sign up for them in time and they were all taken; maybe I wasn't at the library enough. I don't really know.

But I do know that all around were misplaced priorities, usually in this order: (1) Premarital sex/excessive sexual activity. (2) Partying (drinking and drugs are included in this category). (3) Sports, usually football. (4) Social acceptance, usually at any cost. (5) Grades. (6) Graduation. (7) Career.

Note the order. The first three, in my opinion, are recreational activities with little academic redeeming worth. However, I do concede that partying, minus the drink and the drugs, do serve valid functions of socialization and blowing off steam, and I am not against rewarding yourself for achieving some of your goals.

The fourth, social acceptance, is fine, but some students could not draw the line between social acceptance and social slavery, especially in the frats and sororities.

The distinction between grades and graduation is not as strange as it may seem. Some brothers and sisters were not interested in graduation. They only wanted to keep their grades high enough to stay and have a great time at old Suntan U. These folks are on the 10-year plan. At Morehouse, we called them 'Super Seniors'.

I knew some academic success stories in Gainesville, both undergrad and grad. But a 90% failure rate among students of color is just too high.

<u>GET YOUR PRIORITIES STRAIGHT. KEEP THEM STRAIGHT.</u> You are there for one reason: to get your degree and hopefully pick up some

knowledge along the way, and get the hell on with real life. Enjoy all the activities you can during college, but if you screw up, you brought it on yourself.

SUMMARY

YOUR FIRST PRIORITY IN SCHOOL IS SCHOOL.

Proper time management is critical unless you want to spend every hour studying. You should establish a realistic daily schedule that allows you flexibility for socializing, recreational activities, or extra studying.

When it comes to studying, you've just got to do it. Motivation follows action.

Concentrate and repeat.

A study group can be a critical factor in academic success or failure. Avoid lazy study partners like the plague.

If your school allows you to pick an instructor, do research on the instructor before you sign up for the class.

From day one of the class, you must manage your image with the instructor in order to make the instructor feel good about giving you the benefit of the doubt. Image management demands work, prior preparation, desire and motivation on your part.

Remember, school, especially at the administrative level, is a cold-blooded business, with specific rules, laws, and regulations. The school catalog is the administrator's bible. Use it for your own best interests, when necessary.

NEVER, if possible, put yourself where an administrator can use discretion.

Add-drop periods, pass-fail grades, auditing classes, 'get-overs', and incompletes can be used to your advantage to improve your grades. Instructors, on occasion, WILL change grades. Consider using the incomplete/auditing strategy.

Decide for yourself your comfort level of racial interaction in your social relationships. If you choose to socialize only with whites, be ready for the time someone lets you know that you are the exception to the rule ("if every Black person was as smart/dedicated/hard-working as you...", or "I thought you were different..."). These statements are based on a belief (conscious, sub-conscious, or unconscious) in white superiority.

CHAPTER SIX

CROSSING THE FINISH LINE

Success is the reward of toil.

Sophocles

Until now, we have discussed the different things you can do to generally prepare yourself for your academic experiences.

Now we turn to the very specific task of preparing you to take and pass tests, whether true-false, essay, or multiple choice. It is in test preparation that all the separate techniques you have learned (outlining, note-taking, speed reading, memory systems) come together.

GETTING YOURSELF TOGETHER

1. Ask the instructor whether the test is objective (multichoice, true-false (T-F), sentence completion) or subjective (essay or short answer). This gives you an idea of what type of study method to use. For example, group study sessions may be a waste of time for T-F exams because the focus is on knowing facts rather than analyzing and applying them. Be aware, however, that even T-F can be tough, especially if your knowledge of the material is hazy rather than very specific.

You should also ask the instructor whether any special items are needed; blue books, #2 pencils, scratch paper, etc. If so, get the stuff before you forget about it.

2. Spread your exam preparation time over a period of days or weeks, if necessary. Don't depend on 'cramming' to get you over. Probably the biggest mistake students make is waiting too long to begin preparing for the exam. All of a sudden you look up and it's the day before the test. If you have been diligently rewriting your notes and doing a daily or weekly outline, most of this process is already complete. If you have been procrastinating, this is the time that you start to pay for it.

3. Gather all of your study sources together. You should have all class notes, the textbook, your outline, and whatever relevant supplementary sources you feel will be helpful. If you have not completed an outline, go back a few chapters and read how to do so. Do it before you go any further. Your outline will be the primary source of exam preparation.

4. Gather as many sources of possible test questions as you can. Some schools have exam files indexed either by instructor, by class, or by subject. Usually they are found at the reserve desk at the library. If there is no exam file, sometimes either the student government organization or your departmental clubs (i.e. student business association, English club, law student society, etc.) may have files. If they don't sometimes the fraternities and sororities keep test files going years back. If still no luck, ask upperclassmen who have taken the instructor if they have saved old tests.

Then go to the textbook itself. Many have study questions at the end of chapters. Look at your class notes. If an instructor worked a problem out in class, it's a good bet you will see something similar or identical. Did he ask hypothetical, or 'what if'-types of questions that the class had to answer? If so, those questions may form the basis of an essay question.

Look at the syllabus, if you were given one. On what subjects did the instructor place the heaviest emphasis? Does the outline of the syllabus differ from the textbook's Table of Contents? If so, it may give a clue about how the different subjects fit together in the instructor's mind.

5. Go over your outline briefly. No need to study the outline in depth at this time. Go through it to jog your memory and get the intellectual juices flowing. Since you have written your own outline, things should begin to come back quickly.

6. Pre-test yourself, using selected questions or problems. You should not be too neat and formal. Scribble the answers in just a few words. All you're doing now is checking for strong and weak areas.

7. Check the answers, compute your scores and correct the wrong answers. This will red-flag your weak spots.

8. Study your outline again, this time slowly and carefully. This time you should make notes in your mind (as well as on the outline) of weak areas. If you reach an area that is difficult for you to understand, go to your supplementary sources for help (class notes, textbook, outside references). Talk to yourself aloud. This forces you to think about what you are saying. If you can't explain it to yourself verbally, you can't write it on paper.

9. Use the memory system techniques you have learned to memorize formulas, definitions, and lists of groups or concepts. Here, you can use either the Lorayne Link/Peg memory systems or the Hanau system (see Chapter 11 of Hanau's book).

10. Test yourself again. Use the same scribbling method as you did for the first test. Again, check your scores and correct your wrong answers. Depending upon how well you knew the material before the first test, you should have done better on this one.

11. Go over the outline again, concentrating on tightening up your weak points.

12. Test yourself again, this time under exam conditions. Pick out a few questions and answer them under exam conditions. Some people find it helpful to go to the classroom and sit in the chair in which they will be taking the test. Time yourself just as you would in the test. If the questions are essay questions, answer them in the formal essay format just as you would on the real exam. The exception here is when you know you have the writing skills through training (journalistic, advanced English essay, etc). If that is the case, you can answer the essays in a detailed outline format.

Time yourself; write for 10 minutes, and then stop. Then count the words. This will give you a visual idea of how much space you use when writing an essay answer. This will come in handy if the essay has limited space.

Check the answers, compute your scores, and correct the wrong answers. If the questions are essays, be sure to check your grammar and spelling.

13. If you are comfortable with your knowledge of the material, go cool out somewhere.

I believe if you follow this format, you will be prepared for the exam. However, there are several variations of the guidelines listed above that may prove helpful.

Consider having group test sessions. The group can make up a simulated test and have everybody answer and return it at the next group meeting. As you correct it, you can give justifications of the answers. This works great with essay questions and math problems.

The group can also consider giving a mock verbal test. This forces you to articulate exactly what your understanding is of ideas and concepts. Each member can rotate testing the others.

After you have been grilled and tested numerous times, go back to your outline and fill in things you may have missed. Concentrate on those areas in which you have been consistently weak.

Memorize your mnemonics and visualize your memory Links and Pegs (refer to Harry Lorayne's book). Reinforce your knowledge, by reciting them to yourself in the shower, on the way to school, etc. Practice scribbling them between classes or whenever you have a spare moment. Then, when you have put in the time and effort and you feel comfortable with yourself, don't worry about it.

If cramming is necessary: Sometimes you may have to cram for a test, despite your best intentions. If so, you can follow the same format listed above. You'll just have to do it in a lot less time.

If you find yourself in a situation where you are counting down the hours before the test and you have to pull an all-nighter, the best thing to do is to eat early, go to bed early, get up at 3-4 am and study until the test. If you get sleepy, DON'T take a drink; alcohol is a depressant and will only knock you out cold. DON'T do speed or other drugs! That's how drug dependence and addiction often gets started among students. I would not even suggest taking caffeine pills. You can develop a psychological dependence on them. As a last resort, drink coffee or tea to keep yourself awake.

If you are sleepy and your mind is getting fuzzy, go to sleep. Put your head back against a wall and close your eyes for 10-15 minutes. Don't lay down or you can forget it.

WHY YOU SHOULD PREPARE TO CHEAT ON AN EXAM

Some of you will be paranoid about flunking even if you have done everything you can do. You may even consider cheating on the test.

All students, if they are serious about passing exams, should prepare to cheat on an exam. Preparing to cheat is one of the best ways to improve the probability of exam success.

Cheating is far more widespread than most non-students believe. There are a number of preferred methods of cheating on tests, but only four overlapping general categories. You can cheat: (1) before the test (by stealing it); (2) during a test; (3) by yourself; (4) with someone else. I believe most students who cheat do it by themselves during the test, for a number of reasons. One, you don't have to tell anybody. Two, you don't have to depend on anybody else for the correct answers. Three, it's much less risky than breaking into an instructor's office or trying to bribe a secretary into giving you a copy. Four, it's harder to detect and prove if you are skillful enough.

Given the fact that most students cheat by themselves during the test, it follows that they usually cheat by having 'crib sheets', or notes, written somewhere. It could be in a memory calculator or watch, a shirt sleeve or hand, a laptop computer or on scratch paper. Where it is doesn't matter. The most important fact for our purpose is that most students cheat by writing.

When you cheat with a crib sheet, you must, by necessity, condense a lot of information in a few words that will jog your memory. A successful crib sheet must promote understanding; be organized; must summarize the material; and be brief. Doesn't this describe an effective memory system or outline?

I dare you to prepare a crib sheet. You'll find that you won't need it, because the preparation of it has fixed the concepts in your mind! And if you have followed the study/outline/memory procedures in this book, you will be able to prepare a crib sheet from memory. If you can do that, why do you need one?

A QUICK WORD ABOUT CHEATING ON EXAMS

Don't.

TEST TAKING: HOW TO COME THROUGH IN THE CLUTCH

This is it. This is what all the time, effort, sweat, gamesmanship, and perseverance has prepared you for: the exam.

Your final preparation for this moment should have started last night. Now you are rested; you've looked over your outline and gone over your memory system one last time before taking a leisurely stroll or drive to class. You haven't had a large meal today; you've eaten moderately a few hours ago. You've even gotten a little more dressed up than usual to give you a mental lift as you sit in your regular seat.

Finally, the instructor gives final instructions and a few corrections of spelling errors. Strange, but your mind is a million miles away. Suppose what I have studied is not on the test? Suppose I'm in the wrong class?

The instructor comes down your row and places the examination face-down on your desk. How sadistic, you think. Why would she prolong the anticipation? At least she could have turned it face-up.

You turn the test over. What now?

1. Write your name on your test paper. Elementary, but necessary.

2. <u>Take a few deep breaths and relax.</u> It's natural to go into a quiet panic in the first thirty seconds or so. It will rapidly pass. If you have a digital watch with a stopwatch function, start it.

3. <u>READ THE DIRECTIONS!</u> I can't emphasize this enough. If the directions say <u>circle</u> the correct answer, DON'T underline! If the directions say choose the OPPOSITE meaning DON'T choose the SAME meaning! Otherwise, why even bother to study?

4. <u>Scan the whole exam first.</u> DON'T read it word for word, and use some judgment here. It doesn't make sense to spend five minutes scanning a long multiple choice exam if you only have 15 minutes to complete it.

Scanning is important for a number of reasons. It sets your mind for the task ahead by mentally measuring what is required of you. It also allows you to calculate how much time you should allot for each question. You can then look at your exam stopwatch and tell whether you are ahead of pace or behind.

For instance, you may have two hours to complete 20 essay questions. On average, you must complete one question every six minutes. This means that the answers the instructor expects have to be relatively short and to the point, compared to a very long, more detailed answer if you had two hours to answer a single essay question.

After scanning, if you have a bad copy of a test page or a question is unclear to you, go to the instructor's desk and ask her personally. DON'T ask your neighbor!

5. <u>Let your mind flow freely. If ideas or answers come to you as you read the whole exam, scribble them down immediately on another piece of paper.</u> Sometimes you may miss an answer or forget an idea in the mad rush to answer all the questions. Remember, the exam has just started. You have plenty of time, but don't daydream. Don't let any idea or answer get away from you. Many times your first impressions about answers will be correct.

6. <u>Scribble down the formulas and definitions you know you will have to use on a piece of paper, or on a blank area.</u>This is strictly for convenience. If your teacher were to pass by and think that this is a cheat sheet, it would be easy for you to write them again upon

request from the teacher, since your memory system has already locked them in.

7. Begin to answer the questions, easiest to hardest. Answering the easy ones first develops confidence and saves time for you to ponder over the more difficult questions.

Now that you have begun to answer questions, here are some important considerations for answering different types of questions you will probably see on the exam.

TRUE-FALSE QUESTIONS

T-F questions test your knowledge very specifically. There's no room for error. The good news is that you always have a 50 percent probability of getting them right. Here are some suggestions:

READ THE STATEMENT CAREFULLY. I can't emphasize this enough. Too many times, you know the answer but get it wrong because of carelessness.

Don't assume anything. Most true-false questions are straight-forward and not tricky. Don't make the question say what you want it to say, rather than what is printed. Keep it simple.

All portions of an answer must be true if the correct answer is 'true.' If some parts of an answer are true and even one part is false, the correct answer is 'false'.

Long true-false questions should be separated into a series of single true-false questions, if possible. Once this is done, mark the letter T or F by the portion of the question. If you don't know whether the portion is true or false, put a '?' by it. Leave these marks, so when you return to the question you won't have to analyze those portions again. Circle the number of the question, and move on.

If the answer jumps out at you, it's usually correct, but analyze the question anyway. In true-false questions, first impressions are usually correct. But be careful.

<u>Mandatory words like</u> **always, never, must, none, all** <u>are good clues. Questions with these words are usually FALSE.</u>

<u>Words like</u> **often, rarely, sometimes, usually, normally, seldom, or generally** <u>can indicate TRUE answers.</u>

<u>The longer the statement, the more likely it is to be TRUE.</u>

EXAMPLES: Go back to the firemaking passage on pages 66-67. Answer the following true/false questions which are based on that passage:

1. One should always carry matches in a waterproof case on his person.   T F

2. Normally, it is better to build several small fires rather than one big one.   T F

3. In areas with trees, it is recommended that standing dead trees and dry dead branches be used for fuel, and that dry dung or twigs be used as kindling.   T F

4. It is recommended that pine knots and bark be used as fuel, as well as a gas/oil mix, in an airplane crash.   T F

ANSWERS: Question 1 is FALSE. The passage indicates matches should be carried while in remote areas. If you didn't know that, the <u>always</u> was a clue it was probably false. Without reading the passage carefully, you would have assumed that a person should always carry matches, because it makes sense to do so.

Question 2 is TRUE. If you didn't know this answer, the word <u>normally</u> is a clue it was probably true.

Question 3 is FALSE. Here is how I marked it:

In areas (with trees), it is recommended that [standing dead trees and dry dead branches be used for fuel,] and that [dry dung or twigs be used as <u>kindling</u>.]

Dry dung is used as fuel in treeless areas, and not as kindling. Since a portion of this long statement is false, the whole statement is FALSE.

Question 4 is FALSE. Pine knots are used as kindling to start the fire; in an airplane crash, the gas/oil mix is used as fuel.

MULTIPLE CHOICE QUESTIONS

Multiple choice exams (I call them multichoice for short) are tougher than true-false because you have more choices. (No kidding.) They also test your reading comprehension as well as your knowledge. Usually the instructor is looking for the best answer, which is the answer that best responds to the question you are asked. Despite popular belief, most multichoice questions have only one correct answer. Suggestions:

Read all directions carefully. Let your fingers do the walking. Sometimes you may get a group of questions with a different set of directions. Don't gloss over the directions; read them carefully.

The CALL of the question is what you are expected to answer. It is usually the last phrase or sentence before the choices are given. Before looking at the choices, look at the CALL of the question, and circle it. Be careful of questions that have 'except' or 'not' in the call.

If your multichoice question is based on a long, complex written passage, READ THE CALL FIRST. Many times you may have either a long written passage, like our firemaking example, or complicated fact situation in a question. When you finish reading it, you find out that the question you are expected to answer, the call, is so specific that all the stuff you read has nothing to do with answering the question. If it took you three minutes to read the passage, you have wasted three minutes that could have been used to answer more questions.

Save yourself some time by going to the question first. Then when you go back up to read the information, you know what you are looking for.

Work on only one question at a time. If you get to a question and begin to work on it but never finish it, don't worry about it. Analyze it as best you can by eliminating the answers that are incorrect and crossing them out. That way, you don't waste time re-analyzing a question again when you return to it.

Read all the choices before answering. The best answer to the question may be waiting for you further down the list of choices.

Constantly check the number of the question and number you are working on your answer sheet. This is especially important if you are being graded by computer, and when you have left some questions unanswered with the intention of coming back to them later.

Long multiple choice answers should be separated into a series of single true-false questions, if possible. Sometimes the choices are long. That forces you to determine whether the choice is a true statement. If any part of it is false, you know it is not the correct choice. Attack long multichoice questions the same way as the T-F questions.

Use the process of elimination to increase the probability of guessing correctly.

EXAMPLE: We will again use our firemaking example from pages 66-67.

Fire is crucial to survival in the wild because:
    a.   it provides warmth
    b.   it prevents moisture around the campsite
    c.   it scares off animals
    d.   a and b only
    e.   b and c only
    f.   none of the above

The correct answer is (a). This is how I analyzed it:

Fire is crucial to survival in the wild because:
    a.   it provides warmth
    b.   it prevents moisture around the campsite
    c.   it scares off animals
    d.   a and b only

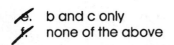

 b and c only
 none of the above

You can get the correct answer by process of elimination, with ju a little knowledge. If you know (a) is right, (b) is wrong but you are n sure about (c), you can eliminate every answer which states that (l is correct. This eliminates (b), (d), and (e). Your probability of succe has doubled from 17% (1 in 6) to 33% (1 in 3). You know that (a) is cc rect, so you can eliminate (f). Your probability of success is now 5C (1 of 2), since only answers (a) and (c) are correct. If you guess (« you are correct.

If, for some reason, you could not make up your mind between (« and (c), you should have circled the number of the question on yo answer sheet to remind yourself to go back to it. If you have marke up the question like I did, you would know that you have alreac analyzed the question once and would not have to waste valuab time doing it again.

If you still have at least two possibilities, here is a hodgepodge hints.

An answer using 'always', 'never' or 'all' is usually wrong. Th answer that grammatically matches the question is usually right. Pic the longer answer of the two when in doubt. If two answers al almost identical except for a word or two, choose one of them. St tistically speaking, answers (b), (c), or (d) are often correct mo times that (a) and (e).

When you don't know enough to eliminate any of the choice always guess unless there is a penalty for guessing. Some experts su gest that you guess strategically. They say you should pick a guessir pattern and stick with it. For instance, if you pick (c) as your guessir answer, pick (c) all the way down and don't skip all over the answ sheet.

Even if there is a penalty for guessing, consider guessing anywa For example, suppose you are taking a test which awards you tw points for each correct answer, and takes away one point for eve wrong answer. If, after using the process of elimination, you throw o all the possible answers except for two, it is now worthwhile for you to guess whenever you can eliminate the choices to only two. This gives you a 50% chance of gaining two points, and 50% chance of losing one point. Take the chance.

ESSAY QUESTIONS

Scan all the essay questions. Decide whether they are short or long answer questions. You can tell by the number of essay questions on the test and the amount of time you have to answer the questions.

For example, if you have 10 essay questions and only have one hour to answer them, the instructor expects short, snappy answers. If you have two questions to do over one hour, the answers should be longer.

If your exam is limited space, you know from practice approximately how many lines you can write in ten minutes. From there, you can figure how much space and time to allot to each question.

Analyze the call(s) of the questions. Circle them. What are you supposed to write about? Go through the call and pick out every piece of information the instructor wants answered. Failure to properly determine what the instructor is asking for kills people on essay questions. If you write the world's best answer to a question the instructor never asked, you still get a zero. Some words in the call of essay questions include COMPARE, which means you should examine the similarities between two concept, ideas, etc.; CONTRAST, which means to examine the differences; DISCUSS, which means to analyze in detail, applying everything possible that you have been taught, from all angles.

Begin with the question you know the most about. Start writing issues, statements or key words you know you'll use in the essay answer.

Write down an outline of your answer. Do this before answering the question. This will help organize your answer. But don't make the thing a work of art. An outline should take no more than five minutes, depending on whether the question calls for a short or long answer.

Example: Suppose you have a two-hour essay exam composed of ten essay questions. That means that you can only spend 12 minutes per question. If you spend 10 minutes on an outline of a question, you are on your way to a C or D, at best, because you will never finish the exam.

Begin writing. Generally, essay answers follow this format:
    introduction (let the instructor know which part of the
       question you are answering)
    historical background, if any
    issues involved
    rules, definitions
    analysis, argument
    conclusions, summary

Refer to the List of References for books that may help you with essay skills.

MISCELLANEOUS HINTS:

• Keep track of your time.

• If you have both multichoice and essay on the same test, answer the essays FIRST, if essays are worth more points. Then do the multichoice.

• If the multichoice and short essays are worth the same number of points, do the multichoice first. If you get caught for time on the essay, you can outline your answer and get partial credit instead of guessing on the multichoice with a 75% chance of being wrong (if the multichoice is the usual 4-question format, and if you don't have time to use the process of elimination).

• Don't back away from the question because nothing comes to mind immediately. Give your mind a couple of minutes to pull something out.

• If nothing comes, go to your memory system and scribble down every issue or topic you've learned in the class. Go through every one until something rings a bell.

• If nothing comes then, make up a question and answer it. You may get partial credit for it.

• If you are rapidly running out of time, take the time to outline your answer in the space provided. Write 'answer outline; ran out of time' so the instructor will know what happened.

BEFORE YOU HAND IN YOUR TEST PAPER:

• Check to see that you wrote your name.

• Check the wording and the calls of the questions. Make sure you answered the questions you were asked.

• Check your answers. Unless you get an overwhelming revelation, leave them alone.

• Make sure you left no blank spaces. Always answer unless there is a penalty for guessing. As mentioned previously, if you can use the process of elimination to get at least a 50% chance of choosing the correct answer, you should seriously consider guessing anyway.

• Check spelling and punctuation.

• Make sure the pages are in the correct order.

• Turn your paper over on your desk and relax for a few minutes, if you have time.

• Unless your mind has come up with a firm answer to another question you were unsure of, turn your test in.

AFTER THE TEST:

• Forget it until the instructor returns it. There is nothing you can do about it.

AFTER YOU GET THE TEST BACK WITH YOUR GRADE:

• After it's returned, get the correct answers either during class time or in the instructor's office.

• Make an evaluation of your exam preparation. If you didn't do as well as expected, determine why, and change your method or level of preparation.

• Continue to work on the instructor, using the techniques discussed in the previous chapter.

SUMMARY

BEFORE THE TEST:

Ask the instructor what type of test you will be taking (true-false, essay, multiple choice, short answer, etc.) so that you can properly plan your study strategy.

Spread your exam preparation over a reasonable length of time so that cramming is unnecessary.

Review and study from your outline. Pretest yourself. After improving weaknesses, lock in the facts using a memory system, and keep testing yourself until you are able to past any test you or a classmate can make up.

Prepare to cheat on the exam.

DURING THE TEST:

RELAX. Put your name on the paper, and READ THE DIRECTIONS!

Read the whole test, unless it is a large multi-choice. Let your mind flow, and scribble down immediate ideas and relevant formulas, factors, ingredients, etc. you will be using.

Examine each clause of a true-false question. If any part is false, the whole question is false.

For multichoice questions, read the call first, and answer the right question. Use the process of elimination, and guess, depending on the penalty.

For essay questions, look at the call, outline and answer the question you are asked, and go for what you know.

AFTER THE TEST:

Check your name, spelling, punctuation. After you hand it in, forget it.

When you get your grade from the test, get the correct answers, evaluate (and change, if necessary) your method and level of exam preparation, and continue to work on the instructor using the techniques you have learned.

I will never say that progress is being made (in America). If you stick a knife in my back nine inches and pull it out six inches, that's not progress. If you pull the knife all the way out, that's not progress. The progress is in healing the blow that the knife made.

Malcolm X

CONCLUSION

Now you have run the race and finished the course. You've accomplished your goals; you've graduated with a degree and a sense of accomplishment that nobody can take away from you.

What are you gonna do now?

WHAT'S NEXT?

After years of structure, concrete goals, timetables and deadlines, many ex-students find themselves at a dead end after graduation. I know that was the case with me; for almost a year after graduation, I flew and drove around the country using some of the money I had left over from my school loan.

After about a year and a half out of school, I got a real nine-to-five job as a prosecutor, which I truly loved, and began my legal career.

'Real' work was a shock. Mainly because there were few holidays, no long summer vacations, and more regimentation than there was in school; suits and ties every day, etc., etc. One day led monotonously into the next. Only by being out of school does one discover how ideal, carefree, and unreal the whole school environment is.

Here are two other discoveries I made that may be helpful to you:

The study habits and the strategies you employ in school, both good and bad, carry over into the work environment. A tendency to procrastinate and then cram during school becomes a tendency to procrastinate and prepare at the last minute for work-related duties. A tendency to organize do research, and not 'reinvent the wheel' before tackling a school-related project carries itself over to work-related projects.

Many of the strategies described in this book are the same strategies used by successful leaders in the business world. Planning, scheduling, efficiency, effectiveness, self-confidence, perseverance, and consistency are all valuable commodities or skills that are always in demand.

In 1986, I walked away from my job as a prosecutor, primarily to write this book, but really to get a grip on my life and to discover what God had in store for me the rest of the way. For the next two years, I was able to devote myself to writing, traveling, and religious study and discussion. I got married in 1988. With all those changes in my life, and after starting a career as a practicing lawyer, it has taken me about six years to write this book.

I consider that time period crucial in my development as a man. After studying and considering Islam in its various forms as well as other belief systems, the most important decision I made during that time was my decision to live my life with Jesus Christ as day-to-day friend and example and the Holy Spirit as counselor and guide.

However, during that time of reflection and retrospection into my life, I found a rough consistency about myself during my 23 years of formal school education.

I, Charles W. Cherry II, have been guilty of committing what may be considered the unforgivable sins; unforgivable sins against myself and against my people.

LOW EXPECTATIONS AND LOW AIM: THE UNFORGIVABLE SINS

Frederick Douglass, bastard son of a white man, who at 16 raised his hand to his master and declared himself a slave no more ... W.E.B Dubois, teacher, philosopher, thinker, writer ... A Paul Robeson, Super man in ebony skin, Rhodes scholar, actor, athlete, entertainer, activist ... Malcolm X, high school dropout, ex-convict, strident, fearless, eloquent voice for militant change ... Martin Luther King, Jr., son of the Black bourgeoisie, preacher, leader, teacher, dreamer ... Benjamin E

Mays, cotton picker to college president, who said the tragedy is not in reaching for the stars, but the tragedy is in having no stars to reach for; not failure, but low aim, is sin ...

NOT FAILURE, BUT LOW AIM IS SIN.

The unforgivable sins: low aim and low expectations.

Douglass; Dubois; Robeson; Malcolm; Martin; Mays; Exceptions to the rule? To many folks, but not to me. Ordinary men who accomplished extraordinary things? Yes. Did they fail? Yes, on occasion. Were they failures? No.

Somewhere along the long road of academia, probably in elementary school, I decided to function on cruise control, primarily because of the fact that I never really felt challenged academically. And in the process, I cheated myself and the people around me.

Frankly, my goal in college was to graduate with a 3.0 average; I got out with a 3.25, which is nothing to brag about. I should have done better.

As I told you, my goals in law school and business school were not to make 'A's or to get on the Dean's List or to make the highest grade in all my classes. My goals were to get the hell out as best I could, and I did, but barely. I got a 2.25 GPA in law school (2.0 is passing); I had a 3.01 GPA in business school (3.0 is passing). I would have gotten better grades if I had known that I really didn't have to work much harder to get them.

Using the system of study described in this book, I passed the Florida Bar exam the first time I took it.

Just think of what I could have done had I set my goals higher, and used the same techniques I have described for you in this book. Rhodes Scholar, international travel, a high-paying job right out of school; who knows?

Coulda; woulda; shoulda. Who wants to go through life using those words?

PRESSURE AIN'T ALWAYS BAD

If you had spoken to my wife Traci, she would have told you that I believe that the four years I spent at Morehouse College were the greatest of my life. I would constantly regale her with stories about the campus life, which for me revolved around the activities of the 'Bloody Psi' Chapter of the Omega Psi Phi Fraternity. I told her some (but not all) of the stories about frat house living; impromptu Greek shows on Spelman's campus; parties; pledge lines; all-night Monopoly, bid whist, backgammon, and dominoes tournaments; verbal showdowns with the Kappas, the Alphas, the Sigmas, and almost anyone else around at the time.

But among all activities I was involved in; the track team (of which Olympic champion Ed Moses was captain); the fraternity; Student Government; the school newspaper: the biggest impact on my life was the peer pressure, in conjunction with the parental pressure, to succeed in school as well as life.

Many nights the brothers of Morehouse: frat or non-frat, freshman or senior, on-campus or off; would talk through the night discussing one question: what we would do individually and collectively to save Black people?

In my humble opinion, the problem with many Black kids today is not too much pressure, but not enough. We older folks, as parents and members of a generation that remembers segregated beaches, firetrap Black movie theaters, colored and white water fountains, outhouses, and slop jars have spawned cultural amnesiacs in less than twenty years time. We have let affirmative action, a Mercedes, a Louis Vuitton bag, Air Jordans, and a 3 bedroom, 2 bath house become anesthetics.

My generation, by its 'don't rock the boat' attitudes, has absolved our young people of their responsibilities to make this world better than they found it. Young folks get the Red Badge of Achievement in today's Black community if they are 15 years or older and are still (1) not a father or mother; (2) not addicted to crack cocaine; (3) not in jail; (4) still in school.

Now, that's understandable in the days of 12-year old mothers, dope - dealing high schoolers and thieves. What happened to the ethic that you are not supposed to get pregnant, use or deal drugs, rob people, or drop out of school? Have we become so drunk with the bitter dregs of modern existence in the last 20 years such that we have forgotten from whence we have come?

And what of our youngsters who get labeled: convict, junkie, unwed mother, illegitimate or bastard child, abused child, special education student, dropout, disadvantaged minority: should our expectations be lowered? And if our expectations are lowered, aren't we committing the unforgivable sin of saying 'yes' to low aim? Don't we have the duty to ourselves and our young people to expect them to reach for the stars? Don't we also have the concomitant obligation to help them to do so?

Brothers and sisters, it is time to put away childish things. Omega versus Kappa; Delta versus AKA; Republican versus Democrat; Baptist versus AME; Christian versus Muslim; East Coast versus West Coast; North versus South; Bloods versus Crips; pro-abortion versus anti-abortion; student versus 'city folks'; your block versus my block.

It irks me when a Black person hires another lawyer instead of me when their decision is not based on reputation or experience or lack thereof, but is based on the last few letters of the other lawyer's name: S-t-e-i-n or B-e-r-g.

It irks me when I go to McDonald's or Burger King and our kids don't know how to treat customers with courtesy or count change without a computer. It irks me when I go to an elementary school, in coat and tie, and our kids say to me "yo, man", when they respectfully refer to a white man in jeans as "Mr."

It irks me to hear of a National Baptist Convention spending millions of dollars at a conference in a city where a Black college was shut down for lack of money. It irks me to go to a national fraternity convention where there are more mistresses, girlfriends, and concubines than wives and families, among brothers who are married, but whe■ a major theme of the meeting is the destruction of the Black family.

My brothers and sisters, we have work to do.

Jesus told the disciples, " who so ever will be great among you sho be your servant, and who so ever will be greatest among you shall b servant of all". Martin Luther King, Jr. followed up by saying that, k giving Jesus' definition of greatness, everybody can be grec because everybody can serve. Said King:

> You don't have to have a college degree to serve.
> You don't have to make your subject and verb agree
> to serve. You don't have to know Einstein's theory of
> relativity to serve. You don't have to know the second
> theory of thermodynamics to serve. You need only a
> heart full of grace, a soul generated by love and you
> can be that servant.

SERVICE? It's about change. Change from an 'I' orientation to 'We' orientation. And where does that change begin? In the immort■ words of Michael Jackson, it begins with the "man in the mirror". If w■ are to continue to survive and finally begin to thrive after 400 years ■ this country, we must again be of service to our God, our husband and wives, our children, our families, and our communities both loc■ and worldwide.

First, we MUST eliminate the negatives. Drop the word "can't" fro■ your vocabulary. Encourage and edify rather than discourage an■ destroy.

Questions: How many of us are trying? How many of us are s■ dreaming? Have our own dreams exploded, crusted over, festere■ sagged, dried up, as Langston Hughes wrote? What individual con mitment have we each made to make life better for someone else■ What actions have we each taken to put our money, time, and em■ tions where our mouths are? And when each of us is finally laid out ■ the hole dug for each of us at the end of our lives, what will be o■ legacy?

Ideally, our legacies should be one of service. Otherwise, the living that we have done has been in vain.

LIFE BRINGS ANOTHER CHANGE

In June 1991, I went to West Africa for the first time with my mother, Julia T., my sister, Cassandra, and a group of Black lawyers (members of the National Bar Association) and their families.

While there, I contracted malaria, a life-threatening illness that kills one million people a year worldwide. In July 1991, I was admitted into a local hospital in serious condition. I was discharged after five days, but was physically incapacitated and unable to work full-time for approximately a year.

The Africa trip and the resulting illness changed my life tremendously.

Within 18 months of returning to America, I had a brush with death, my marriage was in serious trouble, I decided to give up the law, and I had a critical insight into the worldwide effect of racism.

LESSONS LEARNED, 1

There's nothing like near-death to get help you get your priorities in order.

For years, I had grappled with the fact that despite my law school education, I never really wanted to be a lawyer. In retrospect, the reasons I completed my law school education was because I felt that it was the first real academic challenge I ever had, and because my parents were so proud to have an attorney in the family.

After returning to work, it was difficult physically and psychologically to continue to work in a profession I didn't like, but that was paying the bills. The malaria had taken a toll and had left me physically weaker. At about the same time, I came to the conclusion that after almost five years of marriage, the relationship was in trouble. I perceived myself, for the first time, as a failure.

I sought professional help, and got good advice: LIFE IS TOO SHORT

TO LIVE IT FOR ANYONE ELSE. To live for everyone else is another way of committing the sin of low aim by allowing others to control your life for their own purposes. When you live for others, you don't have to take responsibility for your own failures. In your own mind, you can always blame it on somebody else, and you never take the risk of going 'against the grain'.

In short order, I had a shouting match (at age 36!) with my dad about changing careers, made plans to close my law practice, finished this book, and made preparations to file for divorce. I had no guarantee of any income, no concrete plan for beginning another career, a few dollars in the bank, and no woman.

I never felt better in my life. Midlife crisis? Maybe. But who cares?

For you, Black student, the moral of the story is simple: LIVE LIFE FOR YOURSELF! That includes everything: school, love, marriage, work, service to mankind. Live life the way YOU want to live it, rather than the way everyone else thinks you should. And if you feel that you aren't living how you should be living, don't be afraid to make whatever changes necessary to get yourself on track. Just be prepared for the consequences and results, whether they are good or bad. Make the changes and move on.

Is this a mixed message? Can you live for yourself and serve mankind at the same time? Of course you can! Because anytime you serve someone just because you want to or because you see a need without primary motives such as pride, greed or ego, you always receive more than you give.

LESSONS LEARNED, 2

The second major lesson learned was about racism.

A short, 10-day trip cannot make anyone an instant expert on a land as vast as Africa. I know it will take me a lifetime of study and travel to even begin to know the country and its people intimately. (I do intend on going back, despite having gotten sick.)

First, it seems that European civilization has carried an infectious

First, it seems that European civilization has carried an infectious cultural disease, one that Dr. Naim Akbar calls Culturally Acquired Immune Deficiency Syndrome, or 'CAIDS', into any country which Europe has colonized.

Look at the history of world civilization, and witness the wholesale destruction of entire indigenous populations: the Native Americans in North America, the Mayans and the Incas in Mexico and Central America, the Aborigines in Australia, the Amazonian tribes in South America, and of course the Africans. The major symptoms of CAIDS seem to be, first, a sense of self-hatred, of cultural inferiority, which starts out as a small seed planted in the minds of the indigenous population's leadership, that then engulfs the leadership and spreads to the population; and secondly, a pathological greed for material goods, which eventually destroys the cultural and economic equilibrium of the people.

The end result is what happened to those populations, and what Black America is facing right now: a wholesale physical, mental, emotional, educational, cultural, and economic destruction of an entire race of people.

How can CAIDS be cured? In the context of Black people all over the world, we must first learn the truth about each other.

Black America must tell Africa that to be more French, more English, more Dutch, more Spanish, more Portuguese, more Arab; to be more anything other than African, is to betray our common ancestors, to betray themselves, and to betray our children. Black America must tell Africa that America's streets are not paved with gold, but that Black Americans have not taken full advantage of the golden opportunities that America presents. Black America must tell Africa that we are at a critical crossroads in our history, and, in order for all of us to go forward, we need each other in so many ways.

We, as Black Americans, need Africa to help us begin to truthfully resurrect our lost past. Black America must show Africa that we have finally reached a point of intellectual and cultural maturity; that we no longer believe the myth of the noble African savage who had to be civilized, through slavery, by the white man; that whether you use deodorant or not, whether you eat with your right hand, or with a fork, has nothing to do with your worth or dignity as a human being.

Africa must tell Black America, and other Blacks throughout the Diaspora, that Africa is their first home, and that it is time to come back home. Africa must open its arms wide to Black America, and not just for the money, or for the technological expertise that all Black Americans are assumed to possess. Africa must open its arms as a mother would for a long-lost child: not with a sense of pity, but with a sense of love and with an orientation toward the future.

Africa must resist cultural imperialism, in whatever form it appears: computers or other cheap technological trinkets, religion, bank loans, foreign aid, or anything else that is conditional upon changing the positive moral values and culture of the people. On the other hand, Africa must be willing to solve or peacefully allow the tribal differences, the political differences, the religious differences. Africa must be open-minded enough to allow non-native Blacks to participate in solving Africa's many problems. Only then will Africa take its place on the world stage as the mother of world civilization, the home of the Black Diaspora, and the leader of a true new world order.

Both Africans and Black Americans must shake off the mental chains that have made all of us more European than African, the mental chains that allowed another group of people to rename the very soil on which we were born, thus changing the definition of a whole continent. We must get off the 'welfare', whether it comes in the form of foreign aid checks to African countries or welfare payment checks to Black Americans.

Marcus Garvey tried, and America killed his attempt. Malcolm X began to put the plan together, but didn't live to see the day the plan was initiated.

Another lesson I learned is that the educational and technical talent exists, right now, in Black America, to solve the major problems of Africa and America, i.e. living conditions, education, health care, and governmental systems.

In America, there are Black constitutional and international law experts that can put together a system of government, in conjunction with native Africans, anywhere on the continent. These same experts haven't been given a real opportunity to use their expertise here in America. We have Black city planners and engineers, Black building and construction experts, Black agricultural and veterinary experts, Black teachers and educational experts, Black doctors, infectious disease experts, nurses, and hospital administrators.

We have all the necessary expertise for development of true nationhood within the context of African culture and values, and not as a carbon copy of American or European thought and philosophy. We can do it without being permanently indebted to international banks or Western governments. Black people all over the world can, for the first time, begin to realistically think about returning to Africa to help re-develop a continent that belongs to them.

The bottom line: there must be an African solution to African problems. However, the term 'African' must, by necessity, include every Black person worldwide. YOU are part of that solution.

The time is now. With intercontinental air travel; with Africa only six hours from New York; with phone service, computers, international mail, fax machines, audio and videotape, increased mobility of humankind; with an emerging group of post-African independence leadership; with the growing understanding of how important it is for Black Americans to know their history: the time is now. We are the people who can do it.

LOW EXPECTATIONS AND LOW AIM: THE UNFORGIVABLE SINS. Examine yourself. Examine your heart. Make that change. Strive to do your best, for yourself and for those of us who love, respect and need you.

So much work to do! Our people have been wounded in so many ways during our 400-year history of struggle in America. But each one of us, who has been able to achieve more than the preceding generation, is part of the healing process.

I have confidence in you. Your proud ancestors, Douglass, DuBois, Robeson, Malcolm, King, Mays, all committed their lives to give you and me the opportunity to receive a better education than most of them received. That education should eventually be used for SERVICE for the race, and for the world.

This book is meant to make you part of a true 'new world order', by allowing you to receive the best education Western civilization has to offer. So, my brothers and sisters: LET'S GET BUSY!

INDEX

INDEX

APPENDIX

Basic Bibliography
On African and African-American
History And Culture
As Compiled by Dr. Asa G. Hilliard, III
of Georgia State University:

Armah, A.K. *Two Thousand Seasons.* Chicago: Third World Press, 1979.

Counter, A. and Evans, D.L. *I Sought My Brother: An Afro-American Reunion.* Cambridge.

Diop, C.A. *The African Origin of Civilization: Myth or Reality?* New York: Lawrence Hill, 1974.

Diop, C.A. *The Cultural Unity of Black Africa.* Chicago: Third World Press, 1959.

DuBois, W.E.B. *Black Reconstruction In America: An Essay Toward a History of the Part Which Black Folk Played in the Attempt to Reconstruct Democracy in America,* 1860-1880. New York: Athaeneum, 1973.

Garvey, A.J. *Garvey and Garveyism.* New York: Collier Books, 1968.

Hansberry, W.L. *Africa and Africans as Seen by Classical Writers: The William Leo Hansberry African History Notebooks,* Vol. 2 (J.E. Harris, Ed.). Washington, DC: Howard University Press, 1977.

Hansberry, W.L. *Pillars in Ethiopian History: The William Lee Hansberry African History Notebooks,* Vol. 1 (J.E. Harris, Ed.). Washington, DC: Howard University Press, 1974.

176   EXCELLENCE WITHOUT EXCUSE

Herskovits, M.J. *The Myth of the Negro Past.* Boston: Beacon Press, 1958.

Jackson, J.G. *Introduction to African Civilization.* Secaucus, New Jersey: Citadel Press, 1974.

James, G.G.M. *Stolen Legacy.* San Francisco: Julian Richardson, 1976.

Jones, L. *Blues People.* New York: William Morrow, 1963.

Korngold, R. *Citizen Toussaint.* New York: Hill & Wang, 1965.

Price, R. (Ed.) *Maroon Societies: Rebel Slave Communities in the Americas.* New York: Anchor Books, 1973.

Redmond, E.B. *Drum Voices: The Mission of Afro-American Poetry.* New York: Anchor Books, 1976.

Rodney, W. *How Europe Underdeveloped Africa.* Washington, DC: Howard University Press. 1974.

Rogers, J.A. *World's Great Men of Color,* Vols. 1 and 2. New York: Collier Books, 1972.

Smitherman, G. *Talkin' and Testifyin': The Language of Black America.* Boston: Houghton Mifflin, 1977.

Turner, L. *Africanisms in the Gullah Dialect.* New York: Arno Press, 1969.

Van Sertima, I. *They Came Before Columbus.* New York: Random House, 1976.

Vass, C.W. *The Bantu Speaking Heritage of the United States.* Los Angeles: Center for Afro-American Studies, University of California, 1979.

Williams, C. *The Destruction of Black Civilization: Great Issues of the Race from 4500 B.C. to 2000 A.D.* Chicago: Third World Press, 1974.

Woodson, C.G. *The Miseducation of the Negro.* Washington, DC: Associated Publishers, 1969. First published 1933.

JOURNALS

The Journal of African Civilizations. I. Van Sertima, Ed. New Brunswick, NJ: Douglass College, Rutgers University.

Black Books Bulletin. H.R. Madhubuti, Ed., Chicago: The Institute for Positive Education, 7524 South Cottage Grove Avenue, Chicago, IL 60619.

II
EVIDENCE FOR THE AFRICAN ORIGIN OF THE EARLIEST RECORDED CIVILIZATION, FOR THE ANCIENT AFRICANS AS BEING BLACK PEOPLE, AND FOR THE EXISTENCE OF CIVILIZATIONS THROUGHOUT AFRICA BEFORE EUROPEAN COLONIALISM

Adams, William. *Nubia: Corridor to Africa.* Princeton: Princeton University Press, 1977.

Alfred, C. *Art in Ancient Egypt.* London: Alec Tiranti, 1969.

Bain, Mildred and Lewis, Ervin (Eds.). *From Freedom to Freedom: African Roots in America Soil.* New York: Random House, 1977.

Battuta, Ibn. *Travels in Asia and Africa 1325-1354.* New York: Augustus M. Kelley, 1969.

Bell, H. Idris *Cults and Creeds in Graeco-Roman Egypt.* Chicago: Aries, 1957.

ben-Jochanan, Yosef. *Mother of Western Civilization.* New York: Alkebu-Lan Books, 1970.

ben-Jochanan, Yosef. *African Origin of the Major "Western Religions":* New York: Alkebu-Lan Books, 1970.

ben-Jochanan, Yosef. *Black Man of the Nile.* New York: Alkebu-Lan Books, 1972.

ben-Jochanan, Yosef. *The Black Man's North and East Africa.* New York: Alkebu-Lan Books, 1971.

ben-Jochanan, Yosef. *The Black Man's Religion: Excerpts and Comments from the Holy Black Bible.* New York: Alkebu-Lan Books, 1970.

Blavatsky, H.P. *Isis Unveiled: A Master Key to the Mysteries of Ancient and Modern Science and Theology.* Pasadena, California: University Press, 1972.

Bovill, E.Q. *The Golden Trade of the Moors.* New York: Oxford University Press, 1980.

Breasted, James Henry. *The Dawn of Conscience.* New York: Charles Scribner, 1978.

Breasted, James Henry, *A History of Egypt from Earliest Times to the Persian Conquest.* New York: Charles Scribner & Sons, 1937. First published 1909.

Brent, Peter, *Black Nile: Mungo Park and the Search for the Niger.* New York: Gordon Cremonisi, 1977.

British Museum: *The Rosetta Stone.* London: British Museum Publications, 1974.

Budge, E.A. Wallis. *Amulets and Talismans.* New York: Collier, 1970. First published 1930.

Budge, E.A. Wallis. *The Book of the Dead, The Papyrus of Ani.* New York: Dover Publications, 1967. First published 1895.

Budge, E.A. Wallis. *The Dwellers on the Nile.* New York: Dover 1977. First published 1926.

Budge, E.A. Wallis. *The Egyptian Heaven and Hell.* Lasalle, Illinois: Open Court Press, 1974. First published 1905.

Budge, E.A. Wallis. *Egyptian Magic.* Secaucus, NJ: Citadel Press, 1978. First published 1899.

Budge, E.A. Wallis. *Egyptian Religions.* Secaucus, NJ: University Books, 1959. First published 1899.

Budge, E.A. Wallis. *The Gods of the Egyptians: Or, Studies in Egyptian Mythology,* Vols. I and II. New York: Dover, 1969. First published 1904.

Budge, E.A. Wallis. *Osirus and the Egyptian Resurrection.* New York: Dover, 1973. First published 1911.

Carruthers, Jacob H. *Maat: The African Universe.* Unpublished Manuscript.

Carruthers, Jacob H. *Orientation and Problems in the Redemption of Ancient Egypt.* Unpublished Manuscript.

Carruthers, Jacob H. *Tawai: The United Two Lands.* Unpublished Manuscript.

Churchward, Albert. *The Signs and Symbols of Primordial Man: The Evolution of Religious Doctrines from the Eschatology of the Ancient Egyptians.* Westport, Connecticut: Greenwood Press, 1978. First published 1913.

Clark, J. Desmond. *The Prehistory of Africa.* New York: Praeger, 1971.

Collins, Robert O. *Problems in African History.* Englewood Cliffs: Prentice-Hall, 1968.

Cooley, W.D. *The Negroland of the Arabs Examined and Explained: An Inquiry into the Early History and Geography of Central Africa.* Frank Cass and Co., Ltd., 1966.

Cottrell, Leonard, *Lady of Two Lands: Five Queens of Ancient Egypt.* New York: Bobbs-Merrill, 1967.

Cox, Georgia O. *African Empires and Civilizations.* Washington, DC: African Heritage Publishers. 1974.

Davidson, Basil. *African Kingdoms.* New York: Time-Life Books, 1971.

Davidson, Basil. *Discovering our African Heritage.* Boston: Ginn and Co., 1971.

Davidson, Basil. *Old Africa Rediscovered.* London: Victor Gollancz Ltd., 1970.

Diop, C.A. *The African Origin of Civilization: Myth or Reality?* New York: Lawrence Hill and Co., 1974. First published 1955.

Diop, C.A. *The Cultural Unity of Black Africa.* Chicago: Third World Press, 1978. Originally published 1959.

Doane, T.W. *Bible Myths and Their Parallels in the World's Major Religions: Being a Comparison for the Old and New Testament Myths and Miracles with Those of Heathen Nations of Antiquity, Considering also Their Origins and Meaning.* New York: Truth Seeker Press, 1882. Reprinted 1948.

Dubois, Felix. *Timbuktu the Mysterious.* Longmans, Green & Co., 1896.

DuBois, W.E.B. *The World and Africa: An Inquiry into the Part Which Africa Has Played in World History.* New York: International Publishers, 1972. Originally published 1946.

Emery, Walter B. *Lost Land Emerging.* New York: Charles Scribner, 1967.

Fage, J.D. and Oliver, R.A. *Papers in African Prehistory.* Cambridge: The University Press, 1970.

Fazzini, R.A. *Art from the Age of Akhenaton.* Brooklyn, NY: Brooklyn Museum Press, 1973.

Fell, Barry. *America B.C.: Ancient Settlers in the New World.* New York: Wallaby, 1976.

Fleming, Beatrice J. & Pryde, Marian J. *Distinguished Negroes Abroad.* Washington, DC: Associated Publishers, 1946.

Frankfort, Henri. *Ancient Egyptian Religions.* New York: Harper Torchbooks, 1961. First published 1948.

Frankfort, Henri, *Kingship and the Gods: A Study of Ancient Near Eastern Religion as the Integration of Society and Nature.* Chicago: University of Chicago Press, 1978. First Published 1948.

Frankfort, Henri, Frankfort, H.A., Wilson, J.A., Jacobsen, T. & Irwin, W.A. *The Intellectual Adventure of Ancient Man: An Essay on Speculative Thought in the Ancient Near East.* Chicago: University of Chicago Press, 1977. First published 1946.

Frazer, P.M. *Ptolemaic Alexandria.* Oxford at the Clarendon Press, 1972.

Freud, Sigmund. *Moses and Monotheism.* New York: Vintage, 1967. First published 1939.

Graves, Anna Melissa. *Africa: The Wonder and the Glory.* Baltimore: Black Classic Press, P.O. Box 13414, Baltimore, MD 21203, 1961.

Graves, Kersey. *The World's Sixteen Crucified Saviors: Or Christianity Before Christ.* New York: Truth Seeker Press, 1975. First published 1875.

Griule, Marcel. *Conversation with Ogotemmeli: An Introduction to Dogon Religious Ideas.* Oxford University Press, 1972.

Hall, Manly P. *Free Masonry of the Ancient Egyptians.* Los Angeles: Philosophical Research Society, Inc. 1971. First published 1937.

Hapgood, Charles H. *Maps of the Ancient Sea Kings: Evidence of Advanced Civilization in the Ice Age.* New York: E.P. Dutton, 1979.

Harris, Joseph E. (Ed.) *Africa and Africans as Seen by Classical Writers: The William Leo Hansberry African History Notebook,* Volume II. Washington, DC: Howard University Press, 1977.

Harris, Joseph E. *Africans and Their History.* New York: Mentor, 1972.

Harris, Joseph E. (Ed.) *Pillars in Ethiopian History: The William Leo Hansberry History Notebook,* Volume I. Washington, DC: Howard University Press, 1974.

Higgins, Godfrey. *Anacalypsis: An Attempt to Draw Aside the Veil of the Saitic Ises: Or an Inquiry into the Origin of Languages, Nations and Religions.* London: Longmen, Rees, Oras, Brown, Green, Longman, Paternoster Row, 1836. Reprinted 1972 by Health Research, Mokelume Hill, California.

Hull, Richard W. *African Cities and Towns Before the European Conquest.* New York: W.W. Norton & Co., 1976.

Hurry, Jamieson B. *Imhotep: The Vizier and Physician of King Zoser and Afterwards the Egyptian God of Medicine.* Oxford University Press, 1928.

Hutchinson, Louise D. *Out of Africa: From West African Kingdoms to Colonization.* Washington, DC: Smithsonian Institution Press, 1979.

Ions, Veronica. *Egyptian Mythology.* London: Hamlyn, 1965.

Jackson, John G. *Introduction to African Civilizations.* NJ: The Citadel Press, 1974. First published 1970.

Jackson, John G. *Man, God and Civilization.* New York: University Books, Inc., 1972.

Jairazbhoy, R.A. *Ancient Egyptians and Chinese in America.* Totowa, NJ: Roman and Littlefield, 1974.

James, George G.M. *Stolen Legacy.* San Francisco: Julian Richardson, 1976. First published 1954.

Johnson, Samuel. *The History of the Yorubas: From Earliest Times to the Beginning of the British Protectorate.* Lagos, Nigeria: CSS Bookshops, PO Box 174, 50 Broad Street, Lagos, Nigeria, 1976. First published 1921.

Jones, Edward L. *Black Zeus: African Mythology and History.* Seattle: Edward L. Jones, Frayne Printing Co., 2518 Western Avenue, Seattle, WA 98121, 1977.

Jones, Edward L. *Profiles in African Heritage.* Seattle: Edward L. Jones, Frayne Printing Co., 2518 Western Avenue, Seattle, WA 98121, 1972.

Jones, Edward L. *Tutankhamon.* Edward L. Jones and Associates, 5517 17th Avenue, NE, Seattle, WA 98105, 1978 Library of Congress Card #78-61436.

July, Robert W. *A History of the African People.* New York: Charles Scribner & Sons, 1974.

Kandi, Baba Kumasi. *Down the Nile.* Detroit: A Greater Visions Classic, PO Box 21606, Detroit, Michigan, 1978.

Leakey, L.S.B. *By the Evidence: Memoirs 1932-1951.* New York: Harcourt Brace Jovanovich, 1974.

Leslau, Wolf. *Falasha Anthology: The Black Jews of Ethiopia.* (Translated from Ethiopic Sources.) New York: Schocken, 1951.

Lugard, Lady. *A Tropical Dependency: An Outline of the Ancient History of the Western Sudan with an Account of the Modern Settlement of Northern Nigeria.* Frank Cass & Co., Ltd., 1964.

MacKenzie, Norman. *Secret Societies.* New York: Crescent, 1967.

Maquet, Jacques. *Civilizations of Black Africa.* New York: Oxford University Press, 1972.

Massey, Gerald. *A Book of the Beginnings: Containing an Attempt to Recover and Reconstitute the Lost Origins of the Myths and Mysteries, Types and Symbols, Religion and Language, with Egypt for the Mouthpiece and Africa as the Birthplace.* Secaucus, NJ: University Books, 1974. First published 1881.

Massey, Gerald, *Ancient Egypt, the Light of the World: A Work of Reclamation and Restitution in Twelve Books.* New York: Samuel Weiser, Inc., 1973. Originally published 1907.

Massey, Gerald. *The Natural Genesis; Or Second Part of a Book of the Beginnings. Containing an Attempt to Recover and Reconstitute the Lost Origins of the Myths and Mysteries, Types and Symbols, Religion and Language with Egypt for the Mouthpiece and Africa as the Birthplace.* Samuel Weiser, Inc., 1974.

McEvedy, Colin. *The Penguin Atlas of African History.* New York: Penguin Books, 1980.

Means, Sterling M. *Black Egypt and Her Negro Pharaohs.* Baltimore: Black Classic Press, P.O. Box 13414, Baltimore, Maryland, 1978.

Means, Sterling M. *Ethiopia and the Missing Link in African History.* Harrisburg, PA: The Atlantis Publishing Co., 1980. First published 1945.

Morrell, E.D. *The Black Man's Burden: The White Man in Africa from the Fifteenth Century to World War I.* New York: Modern Reader Paperbacks, 1969. First published 1920.

Murphy, E. Jefferson. *The Bantu Civilization of Southern Africa.* New York: Thomas Y. Crowell, 1974.

Murphy, E. Jefferson. *History of African Civilization.* New York: Dell, 1972.

Nyane, D.T. *Sundiata: An Epic of Old Mali,* London: Longman, 1965.

Obadele, I. and Obadele, A. *Civilization Before the Time of Christ.* New York: Dell, 1972.

Olda, Henry. *From Ancient China to Ancient Greece.* Atlanta: Black Heritage Corporation and The Select Publishing Company, 1981.

Oliver, Roland and Fagin, Brian. *Africa in the Iron Age: c. 500 B.C. to A.D. 1400.* Cambridge: Cambridge University Press, 1975.

Oliver, R. and Oliver, Carolyn (Eds.) *Africa in the Days of Exploration.* Englewood Cliffs: Prentice-Hall, 1965.

Osei, J.A., Nwabara, S.N. & Odunsi, A.T.O., *A Short History of West Africa A.D. 1000 to the Present.* New York: Hill and Wang, 1973.

Osei, G.K. *African Contribution to Civilization.* London: The African Publication Society, 1973.

Osei, G.K. *The African: His Antecedents, His Genius, His Destiny.* New Hyde Park: University Books, 1971.

Parker, George Wells. *The Children of the Sun.* The Hamitic League of the World, 1918.

Piankoff, Alexandre, & Rambova, N. *The Shrines of Tut-Ankh-amon.* Princeton, NJ: Princeton University Press, 1977.

Rogers, Joel A. *Africa's Gift to America.* New York: Helga M. Rogers, 1270 Fifth Avenue, New York 10029, 1956.

Rogers, Joel A. *The World's Great Men of Color.* New York: Collier MacMillan, 1972.

Rout, Leslie B., Jr. *The African Experience in Spanish America: 1502 to the Present Day.* Cambridge: Cambridge University Press, 1976.

Samkange, S. *African Saga: A Brief Introduction to African History.* New York: Abingdon Press, 1971.

Samkange, S. *The Origins of Rhodesia.* New York: Praeger, 1968.

Snowden, Frank M., Jr. *Blacks in Antiquity: Ethiopians in the Graeco-Roman Experience.* Cambridge: Harvard University Press, 1971.

Sweeting, Earl, & Lez, Edmond. *African History.* New York: African-American International Press, PO Box 775, Flushing, NY 11352, 1973.

UNESCO. *"The Historiography of Southern Africa: Proceedings of the Experts' Meeting Held At Gaborone, Botswana, from 7 to 11 March 1977."* Paris: UNESCO, 1980.

UNESCO. *"The Peopling of Ancient Egypt and the Deciphering of Meroitic Script: Proceedings of the Symposium Held in Cairo from 28 January to 3 February 1974."* Paris: UNESCO, 1978.

Uya, Okon Edet. *African History: Some Problems in Methodology and Perspective.* Cornell University African Studies and Research Center, 1974.

Volney, C.F. *The Ruins or Meditation on the Revolution of Empires and the Law of Nature.* New York: Truth Seeker Co., 1950. First published 1793.

Walsh, M. *The Ancient Black Christians.* San Francisco: Julian Richardson, 1969.

Weatherwax, John M. *The African Contribution: Parts I and II.* Los Angeles: The John Henry and Mary Louisa Dunn Bryant Foundation, 1968.

Wiener, Leo. *Africa and the Discovery of America.* New York: Kraus Reprint Co., 1971. Originally published 1920.

Williams, Chancellor. *The Destruction of Black Civilization: Great Issues of a Race 4500 B.C. to 2000 A.D.* Chicago: Third World Press, 1974.

Williams, John A. (Ed.) *Y'Bird*, Volume 1, No. 2. 1978.

Windsor, R.S. *From Babylon to Timbuktu: A History of the Ancient Black Races Including the Black Hebrews.* New York: Oxford University Press, 1966.

Woodson, Carter G. *African Heroes and Heroines.* Washington, DC: The Associated Publishers, Inc., 1969.

X, Malcolm. *On African-American History.* New York: Pathfinder Press, 1967.

III

EVIDENCE FOR AFRICAN ANCESTRY IN EUROPEAN POPULATIONS AND FOR THE CONTINUOUS INTERACTION OF AFRICANS AND EUROPEANS FROM EARLIEST TIMES

Read, Jan. *The Moors In Spain and Portugal.* London: Faber and Faber, 1974.

Rogers, Joel A. *Nature Knows No Color Line: Research into the Negro Ancestry in the White Race.* New York: Helga M. Rogers, 1270 Fifth Avenue, New York, 1952.

Rogers, Joel A. *Sex and Race*, Vols. 1, 2, 3. New York: Helga M. Rogers, 1270 Fifth Avenue, New York.

Scobie, Edward. *Black Britannia: A History of Blacks in Britain.* Chicago: Johnson, 1972.

Shyllon, Folarin. *Black People in Britain, 15555 to 1833.* London: Oxford University Press, 1977.

188 EXCELLENCE WITHOUT EXCUSE

IV
EVIDENCE FOR THE AFRICAN PRESENCE IN AMERICA BEFORE COLUMBUS, AND EVEN BEFORE CHRIST

Clegg, Legrand H. *The Beginning of the African Diaspora; Black Men in Ancient and Medievel America.* Los Angeles: Unpublished manuscript, 1977.

Van Sertima, Ivan. *They Came Before Columbus.* New York: Random House, 1976.

Von Wuthenau, A. *Unexpected Faces in Ancient America: 1500 B.C. to 1500 A.D., The Historical Testimony of Pre-Columbian Artists.* New York: Crown Publishers, 1975.

V
EVIDENCE FOR HOW EUROPE UNDERDEVELOPED AFRICA WHICH IN MANY PLACES WAS MUCH MORE HIGHLY DEVELOPED THAN EUROPE AT THE TIME OF HER EXPLORATIONS

Ayandale, E.A. *The Missionary Impact on Modern Nigeria, 1914-1942: A Political and Social Analysis:* London: Longman, 1966.

Chineweizu. *The West and the Rest of Us: White Predators, Black Slavers and the African Elite.* New York: Vintage Books, 1975.

Fanon, Frantz. *A Dying Colonialism.* New York: Evergreen, 1965.

Fanon, Frantz. *Black Sin, White Masks.* New York: Grove, 1967.

Farrant, Leda. *Tippu Tip and the East African Slave Trade.* New York: St. Martins Press.

Hallett, Robin (Ed.). *Records of the African Association: 1788 to 1831.*

London: Thomas Nelson and Sons, Ltd., 1964.

Mannix, D.P. and Crowley, M. *Black Cargoes: A History of the Atlantic Slave Trade 1518-1865.* New York: Viking, 1962.

Memmi, Albert. *The Colonizer and the Colonized.* Boston: Beacon, 1965.

Morell, E.D. *The Black Men's Burden: The White Man in Africa from the Fifteenth Century to World War I.* New York: Modern Reader Paperbacks, 1969.

Nkrumah, Kwame. *Neo-Colonialism: The Last Stage of Imperialism.* New York: International Publishers, 1965.

Rodney, Walter. *How Europe Underdeveloped Africa.* Washington: Howard University Press, 1974.

Rotberg, Robert I. (Ed.). *Africa and Its Explorers: Motives, Methods and Impact.* Cambridge: Harvard University Press, 1973.

VI
EVIDENCE FOR THE AFRICAN-AMERICAN'S IMPACT ON AMERICA SINCE COLUMBUS

Aptheker, Herbert. *American Negro Slave Revolts.* New York: National Publishers, 1943.

Beasley, Gain. *The Negro Trail Blazers of California: A Compilation of Records from the California Archives in the Bancroft Library at the University of California, in Berkeley, and from the Diaries, Old Papers and Conversations of Old Pioneers in the State of California.* Los Angeles, CA 1919. Reprinted R&E Research Associates, 4843 Mission Street, San Francisco.

Blassingame, John W. *The Slave Community: Plantation Life in the Antebellum South.* London: Oxford University Press, 1972.
Bontemps, Arna. *Great Slave Narratives.* Boston: Beacon, 1969.

Brown, William Wells. *The Negro in the American Rebellion: His Heroism and His Fidelity.* New York: Citadel Press, 1971. First published 1886.

Carwell, Hatti. *Blacks in Science: Astrophysicist to Zoologist.* New York: Exposition Press, 1977.

Crummell. Alex. *Africa and America.* Miami: Mnemosyne Publishing, 1969.

Cunard, Nancy. *Negro Anthology.* New York: Negro Universities Press, 1969. First published 1934.

DuBois, W.E.B. *Black Reconstruction in America: 1850 to 1880.* New York: Athenaeum, 1973. First published 1935.

DuBois, W.E.B. *The Suppression of the African Slave Trade to the United States of America, 1638-1870.* New York: Dover, 1970.

Fon, Horsemann, *Black American Scholars: A Study of Their Beginnings.* Michigan: Detroit Balamp Publishers.

Frazier, E. Franklin, and Lincoln, C. Eric. *The Negro Church in America, the Black Church Since Frazier.* New York: Schocken, 1963.

Genovese, Eugene D. *From Rebellion to Revolution: African-American Slave Revolts in the Making of the New World.* New York: Vintage, 1979.

Jay, James M. *Negroes in Science: Natural Science Doctorates, 1876-1969.* Michigan. Detroit Balamp Publishers, 1971.

Kofsky, Frank. *Black Nationalism and the Revolution in Music.* New York: Pathfinder Press, 1970.

Littlefield, Daniel F., Jr. *Africans and Creeks: From the Colonial Period to the Civil War.* Westport, CT: Greenwood Press, 1979.
Lovell, John Jr. *Black Song: The Forge and the Flame, The Story of*

How the Afro-American Spiritual Was Hammered Out. New York: MacMillan, 1972.

Lynch, John R. *The Facts of Reconstruction.* New York: Arno Press, 1969.

Magdol, Edward. *A Right to the Land: Essays on the Freedmen's Community.* Westport, Connecticut: Greenwood Press, 1977.

Marshall, Herbert and Stock, M. *Ira Aldridge: The Negro Tragedian.* Carbondale, IL: Southern Illinois University Press, 1968.

Martin, Tony. *Race First: The Ideological and Organizational Struggles of Marcus Garvey and the Universal Negro Improvement Association.* Westport, Connecticut: Greenwood Press, 1976.

Nelson, Truman. *Documents of Upheaval: Selections from William Lloyd Garrison's The Liberator, 1831-1865.* New York: Hill and Wang, 1966.

Newell, V.K., Gipson, J.H., Rich, Waldo L., & Stubblefield, B. (Eds). *Black Mathematicians and Their Works.* Ardmore, PA: Dorrance & Co., 1980.

Noble, Jeanne. *Beautiful Also Are the Souls of My Black Sisters: A History of the Black Woman in America.* Englewood Cliffs: Prentice-Hall, 1978.

Purdue, C.L., Jr., Barden, T.E., & Phillips, R.K. Weevils in the Wheat: *Interviews with Virginia Ex-Slaves.* Bloomington: Indiana University Press, 1980.

Reasons, G. and Patrick, S. *They Had A Dream,* Vols: 1-3. Los Angeles: LA Times Syndicate, 1971.

Rice, L.D. *The Negro in Texas 1874-1900.* Baton Rouge: Louisiana State University Press, 1971.

Romero, Patricia W. (Ed.). *In Black America.* New York: Books,

Incorporated, 1969.

Singletary, Otis A. *Negro Milita and Reconstruction*. New York: McGraw-Hill, 1957.

Southern, Eileen. *The Music of Black Americans: A History*. New York: Norton, 1971.

Tragle, Henry Irving. *The Southampton Slave Revolt of 1831: A Compilation of Source Material, Including the Full Text of the Confessions of Nat Turner*. New York: Vintage, 1973.

Walls, William J. *The African Methodist Episcopal Church: Reality of the Black Church*. Charlotte, NC: AME Zion Publishing House, 1974.

Williams, Robert F. *Negroes with Guns*. Chicago: Third World Press, 1973.

Willie, C.V. and Edmonds, R. (Eds.). *Black Colleges in America*. New York: Teachers College Press, 1978.

Woodson, C.G. *The History of the Negro Church*. Washington, DC: The Associated Publishers, 1972. First published 1921.

Woodson, C.G. and Wesley, Charles H. *The Negro in Our History*. Washington, DC: The Associated Publishers, 1972. First published 1922.

VII
EVIDENCE FOR THE INVENTION OF "RACE" IN EUROPE AS A MATTER OF POLITICS, NOT SCIENCE, AND FOR ITS EVIL CONSEQUENCES IN AMERICA

Barzun, J. *Race: A Study in Superstition*. New York: Harper, 1965.

Benedict, Ruth. *Race: Science and Politics*. New York: Viking, 1959.

Biddis, Michael D. *Father of Racist Ideology: The Social and Political*

Thought of Count Gobineau. New York: Weinright and Talley, 1970.

Chase, Allen. *The Legacy of Malthus: The Social Costs of the New Scientific Racism.* New York: Knopf, 1977.

Curtin, Phillip D. *The Image of Africa: British Ideas in Action 1780-1850.* Madison: University of Wisconsin Press, 1964.

Gossett, Thomas F. *Race: The History of an Idea in America.* New York: Schocken, 1973.

Jones, Eldred D. *The Elizabeth Image of Africa.* University Press of Virginia, 1971.

Montagu, Ashley (Ed.). *Man's Most Dangerous Myth: The Fallacy of Race.* New York: 1974.

Montagu, Ashley (Ed.). *The Concept of Race.* London: Collier, 1964.

Stanton, W. *The Leopard's Spots: Scientific Attitudes Toward Race in America, 1815-1859.* Chicago: University of Chicago Press, 1960.

Weinreich, Max. *Hitler's Professors: The Part of Scholarship in Germany's Crimes Against the Jewish People.* New York: Yiddish Scientific Institute-YIVO 1946.

Wobogo, Vulinedela. *"Diop's Two Cradle Theory and the Origin of White Racism."* Black Books Bulletin, 4, 1976, 20-37.

VIII
EVIDENCE FOR THE DELIBERATE AND UNCONSCIOUS MANIPULATION OF INFORMATION AND MEDIA TO PRODUCE A "COLORED," "NEGRO," OR "NIGGER," WHO EXISTED ONLY IN THE MINDS OF THEIR EUROPEAN AND

EUROPEAN-AMERICAN INVENTORS
OF THE TRUE BELIEVERS

Baldwin, James. *The Devil Finds Work.* New York. Dial, 1976.

ben-Jochanan, Yosef. *Cultural Genocide in the Black and African Studies Curriculum.* New York: Alkebu-Lan Books, 1972.

Bogle, Donald. *Toms, Coons, Mulattoes, Mammies, and Bucks: An Interpretive History of Blacks in American Film.* New York: Bantam, 1974.

Bullock, Henry Allen. *A History of Negro Education in the South.* New York: Praeger, 1970.

Cripps, Thomas, *Slow Fade to Black: The Negro in American Film 1900-1942.* New York: Oxford, 1977.

Curtin, Phillip D. *The Image of Africa: British Ideas and Action, 1780-1850,* Vols. I and II. Madison: The University of Wisconsin Press, 1973.

Gratus, Jack. *The Great White Lie: Slavery, Emancipation and Changing Racial Attitudes.* New York: Monthly Review Press, 1973.

Gregory, Dick. *No More Lies: The Myth and Reality of American History.* New York: Harper and Row, 1971.

Gross, Seymour I. and Hardy, J.E. *Images of the Negro in American Literature.* Chicago: The University of Chicago Press, 1966.

Hodge, J.L., Struckmann, D.K., and Trost, L.D. *Cultural Bases of Racism and Group Oppression: An Examination of Traditional "Western" Concepts, Values and Institutional Structures Which Support Racism, Sexism and Elitism.* Berkeley: Two Riders Press, PO Box 4129, Berkeley, CA 94704, 1975.

Jones, Eldred D. *The Elizabethan Image of Africa.* University Press of Virginia, 1971.

Ladner, Joyce (Ed.). *The Death of White Sociology.* New York: Vintage, 1973.

Leab, Daniel J. *From Sambo to Superspade: The Black Experience in Motion Pictures.* Boston: Houghton-Mifflin, 1976.

Myrdal, Jan and Kessle, Gun. *Angkor: An Essay on Art and Imperialism.* New York: Pantheon, 1970.

Stoddard, Lothrop, *The Rising Tide of Color Against White World Supremacy.* Westport, Connecticut: Negro University Press. First published 1920.

Toll, Robert C. *Blacking Up: The Ministrel Show in Nineteenth Century America.* New York: Oxford University Press, 1974.

IX
EVIDENCE FOR THE DELIBERATE AND SYSTEMATIC UNDERDEVELOPMENT OF AFRICAN-AMERICANS BY WHITE AMERICANS

Aptheker, Herbert. *A Documentary History of the Negro People in the United States,* Vols, 1-III. Secaucus, NJ: Citadel press, 1977.

Bell, Derrick J. *Race, Racism and American Law:* Boston: Little, Brown and Co., 1973.

Burgman, Peter M. and Burgman, Mort N. *The Chronological History of the Negro in America.* New York: Mentor Books, 1969.

Higgenbotham, A. Leon, Jr. *In the Matter of Color: Race and the American Legal Process: The Colonial Period.* New York: Oxford Press, 1978.

King, Kenneth. *Pan Africanism and Education: A Study of Race, Philanthropy and Education in the Southern States of America and East Africa.* Oxford: Clarendon Press, 1971.

Logan, Rayford W. *The Betrayal of the Negro from Rutherford B. Hayes to Woodrow Wilson.* New York: Collier Books, 1965.

Mellon, Matthew T. *Early American Views on Negro Slavery: From the Letters and Papers of the Founders of the Republic.* New York: Bergman Publishers, 1969. First published 1934.

Purdue, Charles L., Jr., Barden, Thomas E., and Phillips, R.K. *Weevils in the Wheat: Interviews with Virginia Ex-Slaves.* Bloomington, Indiana: Indiana University Press, 1980.

Woodard, C. Vann. *The Strange Career of Jim Crow.* New York: Oxford, 1966.

X
HEROIC SPOKESPERSONS FOR AFRICANS AND AFRICAN-AMERICANS AND WHAT THEY HAD TO SAY

Arnold, Millard (Ed.). *Steve Biko: Black Consciousness in South Africa.* New York: Random House, 1978.

ben-Jochanan, Yosef. *Our Black Seminarians and Black Clergy Without a Black Theology.* New York: Alkebu-Lan Books, 209 West 125th St., Suite 218, 1978.

Blyden, J.W. *Christianity, Islam and Negro Race.* Edinburgh University Press, 1967. First published 1887.

Breitman, G. *By Any Means Necessary: Speeches, Interviews and a Letter by Malcolm X.* New York: Pathfinder, 1977.

Breitman, G. *Malcolm X Speaks.* New York: Pathfinder, 1976.

Cabral, Amilcar. *Return to the Source.* New York: Praeger, 1967.

Cesaire, Aime. *Discourse on Colonialism.* New York: Monthly Review Press, 1972.

Cruse, Harold. *The Crisis of the Negro Intellectual.* New York: William Morrow, 1967.

Diop, Cheikh A. *Black Africa: The Economic and Cultural Basis for a Federated State.* Westport, Connecticut: Lawrence Hill, 1978.

Garvey, Amy Jacques. *Garvey and Garveyism.* New York: Collier, 1974.

Garvey, Amy Jacques and Essien-Udom, E.U. *More Philosophy and Opinions of Marcus Garvey,* Vol. III, previously unpublished papers. London: Frank Cass, 1977.

Hill, R.A. *Marcus Garvey, the Black Man: A Monthly Magazine of Negro Thought and Opinion.* New York: Kraus-Thompson, 1975.

Hooker, James R. *Black Revolutionary: George Padmore's Path from Communism to Pan-Africanism.* New York: Praeger, 1970.

Jacques-Garvey, Amy (Ed.). *Philosophy and Opinions of Marcus Garvey.* New York: Athenaeum, 1974.

James, C.L.R. *The Black Jacobins: Toussaint L'Ouverture and the San Domingo Revolution.* New York: Random House, 1963.

Korngold, Ralph. *Citizen Toussaint.* New York: Hill and Wang, 1965.

Larnson, Peggy. *The Glorious Failure: Black Congressmen Robert Brown Elliott and The Reconstruction in South Carolina.* New York: Norton, 1973.

Maglangbayan, Shawna. *Garvey, Lumumba, Malcolm: Black Nationalist Separatists.* Chicago: Third World Press, 1972.

Martin, Tony. *Race First: The Ideological and Organizational Struggles of Marcus Garvey and the Universal Negro Improvement Association.* London: Greenwood Press, 1976.

Molefi, Kate Asante. *Afrocentricity: The Theory of Social Change.* Buffalo: Amulefi Publishing, 1980.

Nkrumah, Kwame. *Consciencism: Philosophy and Ideology for Decolonization.* New York: Modern Reader, 1970.

Robeson, Paul. *Here I Stand.* Boston: Beacon Press, 1958.

Rogers, Joel A. *From Superman to Man.* New York: Helga Rogers, 1270 Fifth Avenue, New York, 1974.

Walker, David. *Walker's Appeal: An Address to the Slaves of the United States of America.* New York: Arnold Press. 1969. First published 1829.

Williams, Robert L. (Ed.). *Ebonics: The True Language of Black Folks.* St. Louis: Institute of Black Studies.

Woodson, C.G. *Miseducation of the Negro.* The Associated Publishers, 1969. First published 1933.

XI
AFRICANS IN OTHER PARTS OF THE DIASPORA ("THE NEW WORLD")

Bastide, Roger, *African Civilizations in the New World.* New York: Harper Torchbooks, 1971.

Cole, Hubert. *Christopher King of Haiti.* New York: Viking, 1967.

Freyre, Gilberto. *The Masters and the Slaves.* New York: Knopf, 1946.

Marshall, Herbert and Stock, Mildred. *Ira Aldridge: the Negro Tragedian.* London: Bifer & Simmons, Inc., 1958.

Price, R. (Ed.). *Maroon Societies: Rebel Slave Communities in the Americas.* New York: Doubleday, 1973.

Rout, Leslie B. *The African Experience in Spanish America 1502 to the Present Day.* New York: Cambridge, 1976.

Whitten, N.E., Jr. *Black Frontiersmen: A South American Case.* New York: Schenkman, 1974.

XII
DESCRIPTIONS OF AFRICAN CULTURE

Booth, Newell (Ed.). *African Religions: A Symposium.* New York: Nok Publishers, 1977.

Carter, Harold A. *Prayer Tradition of Black People.* Valley Forge: Judson Press, 1976.

d'Azevedo, Warren L. *The Traditional Artist in African Society.* Bloomington: Indiana University Press, 1975.

Jahn, Jahnheinz. *Muntu: The New African Culture.* New York: Grove University Press, 1961.

Mbiti, John S. *Introduction to African Religion.* New York: Praeger, 1975.

Omosade, Awolalu F. *Yoruba Beliefs and Sacrificial Rites.* London: Longman Group, Ltd., 1979.

Shorter, Aylward. *Prayer in the Religious Tradition of Africa.* London: Oxford University Press, 1975.

Wright, Richard A. *African Philosophy: An Introduction.* Washington, DC: University Press of America, 1977.

XIII
AFRICAN CULTURAL RETENTIONS IN THE NEW
WORLD AS AN EXTENSION OF AFRICA

Alleyne, Mervyn C. *Comparative Afro-American: A Historical Comparative Study of English-based Afro-American Dialects in the New World.* Ann Arbor: Karoma Publishers, 1980.

Anderson, S.E. *"Mathematics and the Struggle for Black Liberation."* The Black Scholar, September, 1970.

Anyanwu, Chukwulozie K. *The Nature of Black Cultural Reality.* Washington, DC: University Press of America, 1976.

Christos, Kyle. *Voodoo.* New York: Lippincott, 1976.

Collins, Robert O. *Problems in Africa History.* Englewood Cliffs: Prentice-Hall, 1968.

Deren, Maya. *Divine Horsemen: Voodoo of Haiti.* New York: Delta, 1970.

Erny, Pierre. *Childhood and Cosmos: The Social Psychology of the Black African Child.* New York: Black Orpheus Press, 1973. First published 1968.

Haskins, J. *Witchcraft, Mysticism and Magic in the Black World.* New York: Dell, 1974.

Herskovits, Melville J. *The Myth of the Negro Past.* Boston: Beacon, 1969.

Hill, Robert B. *Informed Adoption Among Black Families.* New York: National Urban League, 1977.

Idowu, E. Bolaji. *African Traditional Religion: A Definition.* New York: Orbis Books, 1975.

Jahn, H. Jahnheinz. *Muntu: The New African Culture.* New York: Grove, 1961.

Jenkins, Ulysses Duke. *Ancient African Religion and the African-American Church.* Jacksonville, NC: Flame International, 37 Longstaff St., Jacksonville, NC 28540, 1978.

Johnson, J.C. deGraft. *African Glory: The Story of Vanished Negro Civilizations.* New York: Walker, 1954.

Jones, Leroi. *Blues People: The Negro Experience in White American and the Music that Developed from it.* New York: William Morrow, 1963.

Martin, Elmer P. and Martin, Joanne Mitchell. *The Black Extended Family.* Chicago: The University of Chicago Press, 1978.

Mbiti, John S. *African Religions and Philosophy.* New York: Praeger, 1979.

Mitchell, Henry H. *Black Belief: Fold Belief of Blacks in America and West Africa.* New York: Harper and Row, 1975.

Nettleford, Rex. *Caribbean Cultural Identity: The Case of Jamaica.* Los Angeles: Center for Afro-American Studies and UCLA Latin American Center Publications, University of California, 1979.

Raboteau, Albert J. *Slave Religion: The Invisible Institution in the Antebellum South.* New York: Oxford University Press, 1978.

Sidren, Ben. *Black Talk.* New York: Holt, Rhinehart and Winston, 1971.

Smith, Ernie. *"The Retention of the Phonological, Phonemic, and Morphophonemic Features of Africa in Afro-American Ebonics,"* Seminar Paper Series No. 43, Department of Linguistics, Colorado State University, Fullerton, February, 1948.

Turner, Lorenzo. *Africanisms in the Gullah Dialect.* New York: Arno Press, 1969.

Vass, Winifred. *The Bantu Speaking Heritage of the United States.* Los Angeles: Center for Afro-American Studies, University of California, 1979.

XIV
OF GENERAL INTEREST

Billingsley, Andrew. *Black Families in White America.* Englewood Cliffs: Prentice-Hall, 1968.

BLACK BOOKS BULLETIN

Davidson, Basil, *Old Africa Rediscovered.* London: Victor Gollancz, 1970.

Doblhofer, Ernest. *Voices in Stone: The Decipherment of Ancient Scripts and Writings.* New York: Collier, 1971.

DuBois, W.E.B. *The Philadelphia Negro: A Social Study.* New York: Schocken Books, 1976. First published 1899.

Durham, Phillip and Jones, Everett L. *The Western Story.* New York: Harcourt Brace Jovanovich, 1975.

Evans, Judith L. *Children in Africa: A Review of Psychological Research.* New York: Teachers College Press, 1970.

Genovese, Eugene D. *Roll, Jordan, Roll: The World the Slaves Made.* New York: Vintage, 1972.

Gutman, Herbert. *The Black Family in Slavery and Freedom: 1750-1925.* New York: Vintage, 1976.

Hammond, Dorothy and Jablow, Alta. *The Myth of Africa.* New York: Library of Social Science, 1977.

Hill, Robert B. *The Strengths of Black Families.* New York: National Urban League, 1971.

Jairazbhoy, R.A. *Old World Origin of American Civilizations: Ancient Egyptian Chinese in America*. London: George Prior, 1974.

The Journal of African Civilizations. Douglass College, Rutgers University.

The Journal of Negro History. United Publishing Corporation. New York: Association for the Study of Negro Life and History from 1916 to the Present.

Kaiser, Ernest. *In Defense of the People's Black and White History and Culture*. New York: Freedomways, 1970.

King, Kenneth. *Ras Makonnen Pan Africanism from Within*. New York: Oxford, 1973.

King, Lewis M. *African Philosophy: Assumptions and Paradigms for Research on Black Persons*. Los Angeles, California: Fanon Research and Development Center, NIMH Grant #R01MH255590-01 May 1975.

MacKenzie, Norman. *Secret Societies*. New York: Crescent, 1967.

Rogers, Joel A. *The World's Great Men of Color*. New York: Collier MacMillan, 1972.

Rowland, B. *The Ajanta Caves: Early Buddhist Paintings from India*. New York: Mento, 1963.

Shepard, Leslie. *Did Jesus Live 100 B.C.?* New York: University Books, Inc., 1967. First published 1903.

Stampp, Kenneth M. *The Peculiar Institution: Slavery in the Antebellum South*. New York: Vintage, 1956.

Turnbull, Colen M. *The Forest People: A Study of the Pygmies of the Congo*. New York: Simon and Schuster, 1961.

Uraeus: *The Journal of Unconscious Life*, Vol. 1 Aquarian Spiritual Center, 1302 W. Santa Barbara Ave., Los Angeles, CA 90037.

Uya, Okon Edet. *African History: Some Problems in Methodology and Perspectives.* Cornell University, New York: Africana Studies and Research Center, 1974.

Vincent, Theodore G. *Black Power in the Garvey Movement.* San Francisco, Ramparts Press, 1976.

Willard. *Lost Worlds of Africa.* New York: Dutton, 1967.

Williams, Robert F. *Negroes with Guns.* Chicago: Third World Press, 1973.

Wilson, Ellen G. *The Loyal Blacks: The Definitive Account of the First American Blacks Emancipated in the Revolution, Their Return to Africa and Their Creation of a New Society There.* New York: Capricorn, 1976.

Woodson, Carter G. *Negro Orators and Their Orations.* New York: Russell and Russell, 1969. First published 1925.

Zaslavsky, Claudia. *Africa Counts: Number and Pattern in African Culture.* Boston: Prindle Weber and Schmidt, 1973.

SELECTED BOOKSTORES WHERE SOME OF THESE MATERIALS MAY BE PUR-CHASED:

Eso Won Bookstore, Los Angeles, CA
Mamie Clayton's Third World and Ethnic Books, Los Angeles, CA
Marcus Books, San Francisco, Oakland, CA
Liberation Bookstore, Harlem, New York City, NY
The Black Book, Baltimore, MD
Amistad Bookplace, Houston, TX
First World Books, Atlanta, GA
Hakim's Bookstore, Atlanta, GA
The Shrine of the Black Madonna, Atlanta, GA
Ellis Books, Chicago, IL
The Talking Drum Bookstore, Portland, OR
Liberation Information, Washington, DC
D.M. Burch Bookstore, Fort Lauderdale, F
Afro In Books And Things, Miami, FL
HueMan Bookstore, Denver, CO

LIST OF REFERENCES

CHAPTER TWO

Daniel Patrick Moynihan. The Negro Family: The Case For National Action. United States Government Printing Office, Superintendent of Documents, Washington, DC., 1965.

"How Blacks Want Japan's Leader to Apologize for Making Racial Slur." Jet Magazine 71 (6): 12-13, October 27, 1986.

U.S. News and World Report: Nakasone (1986); Taifu (1990), page 5.

Joseph L. White. The Psychology of Blacks: An Afro-American Perspective. Prentice-Hall, 1984.

Wiley M. Woodward. "A Slap In The Face." Black Enterprise 19 (3):20, October 1988.

CHAPTER THREE

Marcus Bach. The Complete Illustrated Book of Yoga. Bell Publishing Co., New York, 1960.

Lerone Bennett. Wade in the Water: Great Moments in Black History. Johnson Publishing Co., Chicago, Il., 1979.

George Breitman, editor. Malcolm X Speaks. Merit Publishing, New York, 1965.

Abraham Chapman, editor. Black Voices. New American Library, New York, 1974.

Alice Christensen. American Yoga Association's Beginner's Manual. Simon and Schuster, New York, 1987.

Annemarie Colbin. The Book of Whole Meals: A Seasonal Guide to Assembling Balanced Vegitarian Breakfasts, Lunches and Dinners. Ballantine Books, New York, 1983.

Civil Rights Congress. We Charge Genocide. International Publishers, New York, 1951.

J.M. Dechanet. Christian Yoga. Search Press, London, 1970.

Ellen Irene Diggs. Black Chronology From 4000 BC to the Abolition of the Slave Trade. G.K. Hall and Co., Boston, 1982.

W.E.B. DuBois. The Autobiography of W.E.B DuBois: A Soliloquy on Viewing My Life from the Last Decade of Its First Century. International Publishers, New York, 1968.

John Hope Franklin. From Slavery to Freedom. Alfred A. Knopf, New York, 1974.

E. Franklin Frazier. Negro Youth on the Crossroads. American Council on Education, 1940.

Thomas R. Frazier, editor. Afro-American History. Harcourt Brace Jovanovich, 1971.

Richard Hittleman. Richard Hittleman's Yoga: 28-Day Exercise Plan. Workman Publishing, New York, 1969.

Dick Gregory. James R. McGraw, editor, with Alvenia M. Fulton. Dick Gregory's Natural Diet for Folks Who Eat: Cookin' with Mother Nature. Harper and Row, New York, 1973.

Charles King. Fire in My Bones. W.B. Eerdmans, Grand Rapids, MI., 1983.

Jawanza Kunjufu. Developing Positive Self-Images and Discipline in Black Children. African-American Images, Chicago, 1984.

Jawanza Kunjufu. Countering the Conspiracy to Destroy Black Boys, Volumes 1 and 2. African-American Images, Chicago, 1985 and 1986.

Spenser Logan. A Negro's Faith in America. McMillan, New York, 1946.

Malcolm X with Alex Haley. The Autobiography of Malcolm X. Grove Press, New York, 1964.

J. A Rogers. World's Great Men of Color, Volumes 1 and 2. McMillan Publishing, New York, 1972.

Martha Rose Shulman. Fast Vegetarian Feasts. Dial Press, New York, 1982.

Dennis L. Waitley. "The Psychology of Winning." (audiotape.) Nightingale-Conant, Chicago, Il.,

D.Y. Wilkinson and R.L Taylor. The Black Male in America. Nelson- Hall, Chicago, Il., 1977.

Chancellor Williams. The Destruction of Black Civilization. Third World Press, Chicago, 1976.

Carter G. Woodson. The Mis-Education of the Negro. Hakim's Publications, Philadelphia, 1933.

United States Work Project Administration. Calvalcade of the American Negro. Diamond Jubilee Exposition Authority, Chicago, 1940.

Richard Wright. White Man, Listen!. Doubleday, New York, 1957.

Zig Ziglar. Goals. (series of audiotapes.) Nightingale-Conant, Chicago, Il.,

William Zorn. Illustrated Yoga: Simple Yoga Postures for Good Health and Body Harmony. Wilshire Book Co., North Hollywood, Ca., 1977.

CHAPTERS FOUR AND FIVE

Marjorie E. Aghassi. Getting Good Grades. Prentice-Hall, 1980. Good basic book, especially on test-taking.

Kenneth P. Baldridge. Reading Speed and Strategy for the Business and Professional Person. Baldridge Reading Instruction Materials, Inc., Greenwich, Conn., 1979.

R. H. Bently and S. D. Crawford, editors. Black Language Reader. Scott, Foresman and Co., Glennview, IL. ,1973.

Robbins Burling. English in Black and White. Holt, Rinehart and Winston, New York, 1973.

Ralph and Valerie Carnes. The Essential College Survival Handbook. Playboy Press, 1981. Entertaining (and true) anecdotes included here, especially about the faculty political game.

David R. Claerbaut. Black Student Alienation: A Study. R & E Research, San Francisco. Interesting study taken at a small white private college.

Marva Collins and Civia Tamarkin. Marva Collins' Way. J.P. Tarcher, Los Angeles, 1982.

Johanna De Stefano. Language, Society and Education: A Profile of Black English. C.A. Jones, Worthington, OH., 1973.

J. L. Dillard. Black English. Random House, New York, 1972.

J. L. Dillard, editor. Perspectives on Black English. Mouton and Co., Hague, Netherlands, 1975.

Steve Douglass with Al Janssen. How to Get Better Grades and Have More Fun. Here's Life Publishing, San Bernadino, CA., 1986.

Julia C. Elam, editor. Proceedings of a Special National Association for Equal Opportunity in Higher Education (NAFEO) Seminar. University

Press of America, Lanham, MD., 1983. Great article by Hardeman on Blacks on white campuses.

Irwin Feigenbaum. The Grammar Handbook. Oxford University Press, New York, 1985.

E. A. Folb. Runnin' Down Some Lines. Harvard Press, 1980.

Wilfred Funk and Norman Lewis. Thirty Days to a More Powerful Vocabulary. Funk and Wagnalls, New York. Revised edition, 1970.

Margaret Ann Haller. Essential Vocabulary for College-Bound Students. Arco Publishing Co., New York, 1982.

Laia Hanau. The Study Game: How to Play and Win. Barnes and Noble, 1979.

Peter Kump. Breakthrough Rapid Reading. Parker Publishing Co., West Nyack, NY., 1979.

Donald A. Laird and Eleanor C. Laird. Techniques for Efficient Remembering. McGraw-Hill, New York, 1960.

Harry Lorayne. How to Develop a Super-Power Memory. New American Library, New York, 1974.

Harry Lorayne and Jerry Lucas. The Memory Book. Ballentine, New York, 1974.

Alex Main. Encouraging Effective Learning. Scottish Academic Press, Edinborough, 1980. Good information on how to counsel students on study habits.

Robert E. Morsberger. Common Sense Grammar and Style. T.Y. Crowell Co., New York, 1972.

Maxwell Nurnberg and Morris Rosenblum. All About Words: An Adult Approach to Vocabulary Building. New American Library, New York, 1966.

Peterson and Blackburn. Black Students on White Campuses. University of Michigan, 1978.

Joseph A. Quattrini. Speed Reading Simplified and Self-Taught. Arco Publishing, New York, 1985.

Arlyne F. Rial. Speed Reading Made Easy: Six Steps to Reading Excellence. Doubleday, Garden City, New York, 1985.

Sharon Sorensen. Everyday Grammar and Usage, Simplified and Self-Taught. Arco Publishing, New York, 1982.

S. Stevenson Smith. How to Double Your Vocabulary. Funk and Wagnalls, New York, 1964. Revised by Herbert B. Greenhouse, 1974.

Thomas F. Staton. How to Study. How To Study, P.O Box 6133, Montgomery, AL., 36016, 1968.

Cynthia Ann Blanks Streicher. Effects of Black English on Reading Comprehension. Master's Thesis, California State University, 1984. University Microfilms International, Ann Arbor, MI.

William Strunk and E.B. White. The Elements of Style. McMillan Publishing, New York, 1972.

Helen M. Thompson. The Art of Being a Successful Student. Washington Square Press, New York, 1964.

United States Department of the Army. Field Manual 21-76: Survival Department of the Army, 1957.

Mary-Claire van Leunen. A Handbook for Scholars. Alfred A. Knopf, New York, 1978.

Charles V. Willie and Arline Sakuma McCord. Black Students at White Colleges. Praeger Publishers, New York, 1977.

Harris W. Wilson and Louis G. Locke. The University Handbook. Holt, Reinhart and Winston, Inc., New York, 1966 (2nd Ed.).

CHAPTER SIX

Don Davies. <u>Maximizing Exam Performance: A Psychological Approach</u>. Kogan Page, London, 1986.

Otis P. Froe and Maurice A. Lee. <u>How to Become a Successful Student</u>. Arco Publishing, New York, 1959.

Eric Jensen. <u>You Can Succeed: The Ultimate Study Guide for Students</u>. Barron's Educational Series, Woodbury, NY, 1979.

Abraham H. Lass. <u>Questions and Answers about Getting into College</u>. Pocket Books, New York, 1974.

Adam Robinson and John Katzman. <u>Cracking the System (the SAT)</u>. Villard Books, New York, 1986.

Cliff Schimmels. <u>How to Survive and Thrive in College</u>. Fleming H. Revell Co., Old Tappan, NJ., 1983.

Haskell G. Ward. <u>African Development Reconsidered: New Perspectives from the Continent.</u> The Phelps-Stokes Fund, New York, 1989.

ORDER FORM

Tear out, photocopy this page, or fill in the appropriate information requested below. Send it to:

INTERNATIONAL SCHOLASTIC PRESS, INC.
P.O. Box 238 • Fort Lauderdale, FL 33302-0238
(305) 527-4259
Fax: (305) 527-0223
Credit Card Orders Only!   (800) 'A' STUDENT
(800) 278-8336

Comments, criticisms, or suggestions of other successful study techniques to be placed in the second edition of this book are also welcomed and encouraged. You can write, call, or fax us as indicated above.

< > Add my name to your mailing list. I'd like to know about future International Scholastic Press publications and the availability of lectures, seminars, or speeches in my area.

< > I would like to sell this book in my shop, store, business, or as a fund-raising project. Please contact me with more information.

< > Please send me _____ copies of <u>EXCELLENCE WITHOUT EXCUSE: THE BLACK STUDENT'S GUIDE TO ACADEMIC EXCELLENCE</u> by Charles W. Cherry II. Enclosed is a check or money order in the following amount (No. COD's!):

___ Paperback books @ $13.95 per book: _____

___ Hardback books @ $24.95 per book: _____

___ Add: $2 postage and handling per book: _____

___ FL residents add 6% sales tax: _____

I can't wait 3-4 weeks for delivery. I also enclose the following:

U.S.   First Class Mail @ $2 per book: _____

U.S.   Priority Mail (2-day delivery):
        add $4 for first book, $2 for each extra: _____

Next Day Air:
        add $13 for first book, $7 for each extra: _____

TOTAL: _____

VISA   MasterCard   [ ][ ][ ][ ][ ][ ][ ][ ][ ][ ][ ][ ][ ][ ][ ][ ]   ____/____
                                    CARD NUMBER   Expiration Date

YOUR NAME _____   SIGNATURE _____
(as it appears on card)   (required for credit cards)

I understand that I may return any book within 30 days for a full refund if not satisfied.

Name: _____

Address: _____

_____

ZIP: _____   Telephone: _____

ORDER FORM

Tear out, photocopy this page, or fill in the appropriate information requested below. Send it to:

INTERNATIONAL SCHOLASTIC PRESS, INC.
P.O. Box 238 • Fort Lauderdale, FL 33302-0238
(305) 527-4259
Fax: (305) 527-0223
Credit Card Orders Only!   (800) 'A' STUDENT
(800) 278-8336

Comments, criticisms, or suggestions of other successful study techniques to be placed in the second edition of this book are also welcomed and encouraged. You can write, call, or fax us as indicated above.

< > Add my name to your mailing list. I'd like to know about future International Scholastic Press publications and the availability of lectures, seminars, or speeches in my area.

< > I would like to sell this book in my shop, store, business, or as a fund-raising project. Please contact me with more information.

< > Please send me _____ copies of <u>EXCELLENCE WITHOUT EXCUSE: THE BLACK STUDENT'S GUIDE TO ACADEMIC EXCELLENCE</u> by Charles W. Cherry II. Enclosed is a check or money order in the following amount (No. COD's!):

___ Paperback books @ $13.95 per book: _____
___ Hardback books @ $24.95 per book: _____
___ Add: $2 postage and handling per book: _____
___ FL residents add 6% sales tax: _____
I can't wait 3-4 weeks for delivery. I also enclose the following:

U.S.   First Class Mail @ $2 per book: _____

U.S.   Priority Mail (2-day delivery):
       add $4 for first book, $2 for each extra: _____

Next Day Air:
       add $13 for first book, $7 for each extra: _____

TOTAL: _____

| VISA | MasterCard | ☐☐☐☐☐☐☐☐☐☐☐☐☐☐☐☐☐ | ___/___ |
| | | CARD NUMBER | Expiration Date |

YOUR NAME _____   SIGNATURE _____
(as it appears on card)   (required for credit cards)

I understand that I may return any book within 30 days for a full refund if not satisfied.

Name: _____

Address: _____

_____

ZIP: _____   Telephone: _____

ORDER FORM

Tear out, photocopy this page, or fill in the appropriate information requested below. Send it to:

INTERNATIONAL SCHOLASTIC PRESS, INC.
P.O. Box 238 • Fort Lauderdale, FL 33302-0238
(305) 527-4259
Fax: (305) 527-0223
Credit Card Orders Only! (800) 'A' STUDENT
(800) 278-8336

Comments, criticisms, or suggestions of other successful study techniques to be placed in the second edition of this book are also welcomed and encouraged. You can write, call, or fax us as indicated above.

< > Add my name to your mailing list. I'd like to know about future International Scholastic Press publications and the availability of lectures, seminars, or speeches in my area.

< > I would like to sell this book in my shop, store, business, or as a fund-raising project. Please contact me with more information.

< > Please send me _____ copies of <u>EXCELLENCE WITHOUT EXCUSE: THE BLACK STUDENT'S GUIDE TO ACADEMIC EXCELLENCE</u> by Charles W. Cherry II. Enclosed is a check or money order in the following amount (No. COD's!):

___ Paperback books @ $13.95 per book:
___ Hardback books @ $24.95 per book:
___ Add: $2 postage and handling per book:
___ FL residents add 6% sales tax:
I can't wait 3-4 weeks for delivery. I also enclose the following:

U.S.   First Class Mail @ $2 per book:

U.S.   Priority Mail (2-day delivery):
        add $4 for first book, $2 for each extra:

Next Day Air:
        add $13 for first book, $7 for each extra:

TOTAL:

| VISA | MasterCard | CARD NUMBER | / Expiration Date |

YOUR NAME _____   SIGNATURE _____
(as it appears on card)   (required for credit cards)

I understand that I may return any book within 30 days for a full refund if not satisfied.

Name: _____

Address: _____

ZIP: _____   Telephone: _____

ORDER FORM

Tear out, photocopy this page, or fill in the appropriate information requested below. Send it to:

INTERNATIONAL SCHOLASTIC PRESS, INC.
P.O. Box 238 • Fort Lauderdale, FL 33302-0238
(305) 527-4259
Fax: (305) 527-0223
Credit Card Orders Only!   (800) 'A' STUDENT
(800) 278-8336

Comments, criticisms, or suggestions of other successful study techniques to be placed in the second edition of this book are also welcomed and encouraged. You can write, call, or fax us as indicated above.

< > Add my name to your mailing list. I'd like to know about future International Scholastic Press publications and the availability of lectures, seminars, or speeches in my area.

< > I would like to sell this book in my shop, store, business, or as a fund-raising project. Please contact me with more information.

< > Please send me _____ copies of <u>EXCELLENCE WITHOUT EXCUSE: THE BLACK STUDENT'S GUIDE TO ACADEMIC EXCELLENCE</u> by Charles W. Cherry II. Enclosed is a check or money order in the following amount (No. COD's!):

___ Paperback books @ $13.95 per book: _____
___ Hardback books @ $24.95 per book: _____
___ Add: $2 postage and handling per book: _____
___ FL residents add 6% sales tax: _____
I can't wait 3-4 weeks for delivery. I also enclose the following:

U.S.   First Class Mail @ $2 per book: _____

U.S.   Priority Mail (2-day delivery):
add $4 for first book, $2 for each extra: _____

Next Day Air:
add $13 for first book, $7 for each extra: _____

TOTAL: _____

VISA   MasterCard   [ ][ ][ ][ ][ ][ ][ ][ ][ ][ ][ ][ ][ ][ ][ ]   ____ / ____
CARD NUMBER   Expiration Date

YOUR NAME _____   SIGNATURE _____
(as it appears on card)   (required for credit cards)

I understand that I may return any book within 30 days for a full refund if not satisfied.

Name: _____

Address: _____

_____

ZIP: _____   Telephone: _____

ORDER FORM

Tear out, photocopy this page, or fill in the appropriate information requested below. Send it to:

INTERNATIONAL SCHOLASTIC PRESS, INC.
P.O. Box 238 • Fort Lauderdale, FL 33302-0238
(305) 527-4259
Fax: (305) 527-0223
Credit Card Orders Only! (800) 'A' STUDENT
(800) 278-8336

Comments, criticisms, or suggestions of other successful study techniques to be placed in the second edition of this book are also welcomed and encouraged. You can write, call, or fax us as indicated above.

< > Add my name to your mailing list. I'd like to know about future International Scholastic Press publications and the availability of lectures, seminars, or speeches in my area.

< > I would like to sell this book in my shop, store, business, or as a fund-raising project. Please contact me with more information.

< > Please send me _____ copies of <u>EXCELLENCE WITHOUT EXCUSE: THE BLACK STUDENT'S GUIDE TO ACADEMIC EXCELLENCE</u> by Charles W. Cherry II. Enclosed is a check or money order in the following amount (No. COD's!):

___ Paperback books @ $13.95 per book: _____
___ Hardback books @ $24.95 per book: _____
___ Add: $2 postage and handling per book: _____
___ FL residents add 6% sales tax: _____
I can't wait 3-4 weeks for delivery. I also enclose the following:

U.S.   First Class Mail @ $2 per book: _____

U.S.   Priority Mail (2-day delivery):
      add $4 for first book, $2 for each extra: _____

Next Day Air:
      add $13 for first book, $7 for each extra: _____

TOTAL: _____

VISA   **MasterCard**   [| | | | | | | | | | | | | | | | |]   ___/___
                               CARD NUMBER   Expiration Date

YOUR NAME _____   SIGNATURE _____
(as it appears on card)   (required for credit cards)

I understand that I may return any book within 30 days for a full refund if not satisfied.

Name: _____

Address: _____

_____

ZIP: _____   Telephone: _____